MURTY CLASSICAL
LIBRARY OF INDIA

BIHARILAL
HE SPOKE OF LOVE

T0335275

MURTY CLASSICAL LIBRARY OF INDIA

Sheldon Pollock, General Editor

Editorial Board
Francesca Orsini
Sheldon Pollock
David Shulman

BIHARILAL

HE SPOKE OF LOVE
Selected Poems from the Satsai

Translated by
RUPERT SNELL

MURTY CLASSICAL LIBRARY OF INDIA
HARVARD UNIVERSITY PRESS
Cambridge, Massachusetts
London, England
2022

Copyright © 2021 by the President and Fellows of Harvard College
All rights reserved
Printed in the United States of America
First printing

First published in Murty Classical Library of India,
Volume 27, Harvard University Press, 2021.

SERIES DESIGN BY M9DESIGN

Library of Congress Cataloging-in-Publication Data

Names: Bihari Lal, 1595-1663, author. |
Snell, Rupert, translator. |
Container of (expression): Bihari Lal, 1595-1663. Satasaī. |
Container of (expression): Bihari Lal, 1595-1663. Satasaī. English. |
Title: Poems from the Satsai / Biharilal ; translated by Rupert Snell.
Other titles: Murty classical library of India ; 27.
Description: Cambridge, Massachusetts :
Harvard University Press, 2021.
Series: Murty classical library of India ; 27 |
English.
Includes bibliographical references.
Identifiers: LCCN 2020010100 |
ISBN 9780674268746 (pbk.)
Subjects: LCSH: Braj poetry—1500-1800—History and criticism.
Classification: LCC PK1967.9.V47 S2713 2021 |
DDC 891.4/312--dc23
LC record available at https://lccn.loc.gov/2020010100

CONTENTS

INTRODUCTION

The Poet Biharilal

Biharilal (known also as Biharidas and simply as Bihari) was born about 1600 C.E., and although he inhabited a historical period that is now usually called the early modern, his poetry belongs to genres reaching back for hundreds of years and is nothing if not traditional. He composed his *Satsaī* (Seven Hundred Poems) in the early or middle years of the seventeenth century under the courtly patronage of Jai Singh Mirza of Amber (Amer) in Rajasthan. Though we know little more of Bihari's biography than this, his poetry is a confluence of acuity, tenderness, and artistic creativity. He writes about love and beauty, and about the condition of those who fall victim to both or either.

As we might expect with a text beginning with the personal pronoun *merī* ("my"), a careful reading gives us real insights into the character of the poet. Of his outer life, however, we know little more than this bare sketch penned by R. S. McGregor: "Bihārīlāl, a Caturvedī (Caube) brahman, was born most probably at or near Gwalior around the year 1600. His father, Keśavrāy, was a fine poet. Tradition ascribes to Bihārīlāl periods of residence at Vrindaban and at Agra in early life; what is certain is that he became a dependant of king Jaysiṃh [Jai Singh] Mīrzā of Amber (Jaypur [*sic*]: 1617–67)."[1]

Literary historians have tried to cut through the accretions of legend to find the provable essentials of Bihari's life. But at the same time they have been eager to promote the status of this most admired poet, and hence have been loath to depart too far from the received biography, which is hagiographical in tone and purpose. Accounts of Bihari's circumstances related by even the most respected Hindi-medium literary studies are based on sources that collapse under the lightest interrogation, and we lack any hard data on which a reliable life of Biharilal could be constructed. In his wide-ranging work *Kavivar Bihārī* (The great poet Bihari), the celebrated Bihari scholar Jagannathdas "Ratna-kar" unwittingly exemplifies this dilemma. On the one hand, he favors a commonsense discrimination of the plausible from the implausible as he sifts and evaluates various quotations from commentaries and other sources; on the other, he proceeds to relate an explicit version of Bihari's life that even purports to record individual conversations and is generally marked by an almost fairy-tale naïveté.[2]

At the core of the traditional version of Bihari's life is a brief verse biography in forty-eight couplets, the anonymous *Bihārī-bihāra* (Bihari's Roamings, or rather "A Rambler's Amble").[3] The *Bihārī-bihāra* recounts the main elements of the received biography, though it is impossible to say whether this is the original source or merely a compendium of legendary material. The text, written in the first person, gives an account of Bihari's life that may be summarized as follows:

Bihari was born on Wednesday, the eighth day of the light fortnight of the month of Karttik, V.S. 1654 [1597

C.E.], in Madhupuri (Mathura). His father was Keshav-dev, a Chaube brahman; his grandfather, Vasudev. At some time, Bihari's parents came to Vrindaban, and Bihari studied Sanskrit and his own vernacular as well as music and other subjects. The emperor Shah Jahan, visiting Vrindaban, was sufficiently impressed by Bihari's music[4] and poetry to invite him to court at Argalpur (Agra). There he recited *ghazals,* songs, and poetry to the emperor; and on the day when Shah Jahan's son was born, Bihari was called upon to recite verse to an assembly of fifty-two kings of India. The poet was rewarded with an annual stipend. He later visited the Mirza Raja of Amber, called Jai Singh or Jai Shah and known as a brilliant warrior. Initially, Bihari had no access to Jai Singh, and the royal servants would not intercede for him; he languished unregarded for two full months. But when Jai Singh became obsessed with a young queen or concubine and began ignoring affairs of state, Bihari wrote a poem [see verse 26] that was laid in Jai Singh's bedchamber; this brought the king to his senses. Jai Singh rewarded Bihari and commissioned more verses; each couplet earned him a gold coin, prompting his aspirations, and after completing the work within two months, Bihari took permission to leave the city. A bond of love drew him to Vrindaban, the center of Krishna worship. He wrote poetry for many other kings, but nowhere found the respect he had known at Jai Singh's court. Losing his taste for poetry, he took to the devotional life: "Bihari Lal" became "Bihari Das," the date of this renunciation of the world being Monday, the seventh day after the new moon of the month Madhumasa (Chaitra), V.S. 1742 (1685 C.E.).

The autobiographical mode of the first-person narrative is belied by the banal tone of the verses: had he written his own story, the master poet Bihari would surely have achieved something more sophisticated than the markedly humdrum account summarized in translation here. (Indeed, it might be asked why someone who has self-confessedly renounced the world would indulge in autobiography at all, especially given the lack of an autobiographical tradition in Indian literature of that period.)[5] Furthermore, the chronologies expressed in the text are not borne out by almanacs of the years concerned.[6] For insight into Bihari's poetry, therefore, we must turn inward to the evidence of the text itself; but this requires first knowing something about the language in which it was composed.

Braj Bhasha as a Literary Language

Braj Bhasha is the language of the Braj region, located a hundred miles to the south of Delhi.[7] Places of pilgrimage within this locale, such as Vrindaban, Mathura, Govardhan Hill, and the Yamuna River, have long been associated with the Krishna narrative that forms a major current in the devotional tradition known as bhakti, which involves emotionally charged worship of the godhead. Through this Krishna connection, the supposedly rustic regional dialect of Braj Bhasha came to engender a prolific vernacular literature anchored in Krishna narratives. From approximately the fifteenth century, local traditions of folk song and popular hymnody were grafted onto the classical heritage of Krishna lore inherited from the Sanskrit Puranas, producing many interrelated genres of poetry. The bucolic setting of Krishna's childhood and adolescence in fondly imagined riverside groves touched Braj Bhasha with sweetness, while its performance in song tinged it with a unique musicality and lyricism (and to this day, the lyrics of Hindustani music—the north Indian tradition—are imbued with this language). In the sixteenth century, vernacular Krishna poetry reached such an ascendancy that the Braj dialect became generalized for literary purposes far from the Braj homeland and its Krishna narrative; until the Delhi dialect of Khari Boli began, in the nineteenth century, to prevail in a movement toward modernity and a growing sense of national identity, Braj Bhasha held sway as the poetic dialect par excellence right across the so-called Hindi belt of northern India.

The History and Structure of the Satsaī

The Braj Bhasha of the *Satsaī* is a literary construct, heavily influenced by the Sanskrit textual tradition but also replete with loanwords from Persian and Arabic, reflecting the influence of Mughal culture on the Rajput courts.[8] And just as the language itself owes a great debt to its Sanskritic forebears, so too the tropes of the poetry derive very largely from devotional and courtly genres of earlier centuries. A particularly potent and beloved trope is the bittersweet sorrow of "love in separation" (*viraha*), which forms one of the main themes of Bihari's *Satsaī:*

> Your absence is a rare and matchless fire:
> it flourishes in monsoon rains.
> No waterfall, oh Lal, can douse its blaze.[9]

The poems thrive on inference, and this one rests on the interpretation of the rainy season as a cruel time when separated lovers must *remain* separated, travel being impossible; a further trope is that of the paradox, in which the lover's burning passion is inflamed rather than extinguished by rainfall. Rather than grouping them thematically, most recensions of Bihari's text present the poems in an apparently random order, allowing themes such as *viraha* to rub shoulders with lush descriptions of the heroine, caustic comments on rustic philistinism, praise of a royal patron, aphoristic statements on life generally, or observations on God's shameful failure to fulfill his mandate as savior in a troubling world.

Most of the conventions, themes, meters, and sentiments found in the text have their roots in earlier literature. The title *Satsaī,* perhaps bestowed by a compiler rather than by the poet himself, derives from the Prakrit word *sattasaī,* which in turn reflects the Sanskrit *saptaśatī;* the meaning is "seven hundred," or "seven centuries," referring to the notional number of individual couplets constituting such a work. Many Indic texts have such numerical names, typically indicating a collection of independent stanzas whose disparate contents do not yield a descriptive title; Braj Bhasha itself boasts a number of *Satsaīs,* each a collection of poems on a set of themes, and Bihari's is among the first. The closest model for his *Satsaī,* however, is from a much earlier time: it is the Prakrit *Sattasaī* perhaps compiled (and partly composed?) by a monarch called Hala, who lived and ruled in the Andhra area of south India at some time in the early centuries of the Common Era.[10]

Several of Bihari's couplets reflect models to be found in Hala's compilation, and an example using a literal English prose translation and a contemporary English verse rendering will serve to show the depth of field behind the conventions of Braj Bhasha poetry. The English prose translation:

> Oh traveller! Look here—in the mid-day even the shadow (of a man) does not slightly come out, lying hidden under the body (itself), out of fear of the Sun's heat. Why should you not then take rest (in our house)?[11]

A contemporary English verse translation by the poet Arvind Krishna Mehrotra humanizes the poem and makes it more comprehensible:

> Afraid of midday heat,
>   Even your shadow
> Stays under your feet:
>   Come into the shade, traveller.[12]

The substance may seem slight, but a well-attuned reader approaching the Prakrit poem with a sympathetic knowledge of its conventions would find much more here than some inconsequential chat about the weather. The poem's significance lies in an implied subtext, and the words themselves are the tip of an (unseasonal!) iceberg of meaning. The "traveller" is an actual or potential or imagined lover, and the speaker is an enamored woman who uses the summer heat as a pretext to lure him into her house. The references to "shadows" and "bodies" have a double purpose: they make a naturalistic poetic observation of the fact that shadows shrink to nothing at high noon, while their physicality hints at the sensual implication of the female speaker's words—hinting that "I would like to be where that shadow is, under your body." No names or other details attach to the protagonists, though neighboring couplets may add missing detail, deepening the reader's insight into their experiential world. The intimate symbolic connection between landscape and human relations runs deep within the poetry.

The same conceit of "shadows shrinking away at noon" appears in a couplet from Bihari's *Satsaī*:

> Settling within the dense wood,
> lurking deep within the house: at summer's noon,
> even shadow seeks shade.[13]

Like its Prakrit model, the Braj poem only *implies* the speaker's romantic intention (without which either couplet would be little more than a high-temperature pastoral), but Bihari hides the inference even more deeply, going so far as to omit even the traveler from the tale. Thus the task of understanding an individual poem is made possible only by the reader's familiarity with such conceits and by the broader context of the genre as a whole. Each stanza in a text of this kind helps contextualize and explain all the others.

If Bihari subtracts from the poem's content by dropping the traveler, he adds to its depth with new allusions reflective of Braj poetics. First, his reference to the "dense wood" evokes the bucolic environment and lush setting of Radha-Krishna trysts—a narrative habitat that features very commonly in early modern vernacular poetry, as we shall see below. Second, the poem makes specific mention of the summer month Jeth, hinting at another medieval genre postdating Hala, namely the vernacular "song of the twelve months" in which romantic conceits such as the laments of separated lovers are projected onto the modulating backdrop of the annual calendar. Third, the personification of the summer heat, incipient in the Prakrit poem, where the verb "hide" suggests a sentient subject rather than an inanimate one, is taken further by Bihari with verbs such as "to settle" and "to want or seek." And fourth, Bihari's couplet uses alliteration in ways typical of Braj poetics, for example in bringing a cohesion to the final quarter of the poem, "even shade desires shade" (*chã̄hau cāhati chã̄ha*), foregrounding it as a kind of punchline or key to the verse as a whole. Since the aesthetic effect of poetry derives as much from such finely worked-out effects as from the raw materials of its basic conceits, Bihari's poems are very much more than mere derivative copies of earlier originals: the vibrancy of a poem derives from its present detail rather than its past history.

Radha and Krishna as Hero and Heroine

The amorous narratives of Radha and Krishna loom large in the *Satsaī*, and although only about a tenth of the seven hundred couplets mention these protagonists by name, retailers of the text—commentators and artists alike—often read them into the action throughout. The *Satsaī* is essentially a conflation of two tropes: Radha-Krishna narratives in their bucolic Braj setting, and a set of stylized "hero and heroine" motifs inherited from Sanskrit and Prakrit forebears. For the most part, individual couplets separate the two tropes of devotional and courtly or human love, as shown respectively in the following two examples:

His body blends with shadow, hers with moon;
two souls are one, as Hari and Radha
roam the lane.[14]

On the festival of Teej, her rivals dressed in finest garb
and gems; but how their faces crumpled when they saw
her rumpled clothes.[15]

The first of these two couplets, reflecting the divine sport of Hari (Krishna) and Radha in the groves of Braj, would not be out of place in a wholeheartedly devotional work; the second portrays love rivalries typical of ancient Indian poetical texts, including the *Saptaśatī* tradition. But the following couplet conflates these two genres and has Shyam (Krishna) appear on the stage of a courtly drama:

> Seeing her in company, Shyam touched a lotus
> to his brow; she caught him in her mirror ring
> and held him to her heart.[16]

This drawing together of two narrative strands is not the work of Bihari alone but reflects the poetic interests of the so-called Rīti school of Braj Bhasha poetry, a type of aesthetic movement developed primarily by court poets in the seventeenth century. Here, revisited stylized tropes of categories of hero-and-heroine poetry merge with genres of Krishna poetry that had developed in the first major flowering of Braj Bhasha verse in the sixteenth century.

The heroine, then, is a plural or composite figure. As we have seen, she may be Radha, drawn from bhakti narratives; or she may be any one of a cast of time-honored rhetorical types such as "she whose husband is abroad", "she who has elaborately prepared for the arrival of the lover", or the "victim of unfaithfulness".[17] Fair of countenance, she outshines the moon and is invisible in moonlight, though her presence is betrayed by her own fragrance; if her fair face does not lighten night's darkness, her teeth certainly will when she smiles; her fairness contrasts with Krishna's dusky coloring—for if the beloved is Radha, then the lover is Krishna. Gold is invisible against the fair skin of the heroine but is revealed by touch; a forehead mark of sandalwood that blends invisibly with her brow stands out when her skin is flushed with wine, and her white jasmine garland shows up on her chest when it withers and darkens. Thus she is innately superior to all the standard objects of comparison;

the circumstances of these events—the touching of skin, the drinking of wine, the night-withering of flowers—all bear an erotic charge, and indeed such implicit components are often the "point" of the poems.

So slender is the heroine that the very existence of her waist is a matter of philosophical speculation; so extreme is her beauty that the inadequacy of conventional descriptive tropes itself becomes a conventional trope. Her eyes shoot coquettish arrow glances from arched brow bows. Juliet-like,[18] she may be on the cusp of maturity, blending girlhood with adolescent ripeness, but she becomes a consummate lover, adept in the "superior position." The agony of *viraha,* or love-in-separation, threatens her sanity and her life. It makes her burn with a passionate heat that even affects the local microclimate; once-happy associations now seem to her like torture, and the cooling moon scorches her.

Meetings of lover and beloved have to be contrived amid conservative social restrictions, with family elders being a particular impediment (though a husband's handsome younger brother may divert a young wife); fortunately, much can be communicated by a touch or a stolen glance, and the village setting offers potential for many fleeting encounters. Tall-standing crops make convenient trysting places—at least until harvest time. Jealous rivalries abound between co-wives striving for their shared husband's attentions, especially when a young bride joins the household, a dangerous moment for her aging rivals. Love is often personified, especially as the love god Kamdev. A favorite technique is that of the tableau, a descriptive sketch frozen in time like a still shot in a movie, which makes the short couplet echo long in the mind.

When offended by her lover's faithlessness, the heroine sulks with a jealous anger that her female companions, the *sakhīs*, or go-betweens, are hard pressed to overcome. Meanwhile the *sakhīs* delight in noting the poorly concealed physical evidence of the lovers' clandestine escapades. Many couplets are open to several interpretations—is the heroine describing herself, or is a *sakhī* describing her?—and although this multivalency is essential to opening up the poetic potency of the couplets, the commentators see it as their responsibility to close it down, specifying the dramatis personae and silencing much of the semantic echo that lies at the heart of the poetic principle.

God's various roles include that of savior, and he may be chastised for failing in his supposed duty as remover of suffering; hence the occasional derogation of the divine. In a more mundane setting, many couplets read like occasional poems from the royal court, perhaps deflating pretentiousness or targeting some courtly occurrence of hubris, boorishness, or other human folly. Bihari's role as court poet is also seen in a handful of encomiums to his patron, Jai Shah; at least one couplet refers to his famous mirror-work room that tourists can still peer into— though no longer enter—in the palace at Amber. But these panegyrics seem a little dutiful, like tears forced to an actor's eye, suggesting that a laureate role may confine or chafe the creative spirit, or simply fail to inspire it.

Is the Satsaī a "Devotional" Work?

As the discussion so far would lead us to expect, the greatest "pun" in the serious-but-playful *Satsaī* is its simultaneous reference to worldliness and divinity. Although the commentators, in their tireless rote, strive to tease apart the various strands of meaning, the *Satsaī's* tapestry is at its most resplendent when these different modes interweave freely. Devotional immanence and human experience are the warp and woof of its fabric.[19] To separate the different modes of love in which sentiment inheres is to tamper with the very mechanisms of its delivery. This is the poetry of the loving spirit, and love knows no bounds.

The *Satsaī* combines ancient tropes from Sanskritic poetry with Krishna bhakti narratives from such texts as the approximately tenth-century *Bhāgavata Purāṇa* (The Purana of the Lord)[20] and—newly featuring Radha—the twelfth-century *Gītagovinda* (The Song of Govinda).[21] These Sanskrit texts had spawned countless vernacular retellings well before Bihari's time, and in poetry of the Rīti school a broadening of the narrative allowed Radha and Krishna to step out of their usual habitation in Vrindaban's groves to become the archetypical hero and heroine in a wider field of love poetry. Thus although, as already noted, few of Bihari's poems name Krishna or Radha specifically, manuscript paintings regularly portray the hero and heroine in the standard iconography of the divine couple; and commentators tend to follow suit in their interpretations. When a poem describes a riverbank tryst under an autumn moon, who is to say that the unnamed hero and heroine are not this familiar pair? And when a poet invokes the agelessly appealing theme of *viraha*—the agony of separation from a beloved—who is to say whether the context is a "merely" romantic one or an expression of the soul's yearning for God? Traditional critical taxonomies thrive on clear distinctions of context, but a latent ambiguity in the meaning of things is surely a characteristic of true art, and Bihari's skill exploits this to the full. To gain as rich as possible an appreciation of his poetry, therefore, we need to be open to the widest possible range of its meanings, and to be sensitive to its music.[22] Let us read a connected pair of his finest poems:

How shall Hari gain the chamber of my heart
while falsehood's latch and bolt
lock tight the door?[23]

Awakening, I see the door still chained.
Then who can say how he comes in
and vanishes again?[24]

The two poems share rhyme words and a "locked door" motif, while a shared interrogative mood gives them both a questioning wonderment.[25] But a subtler kind of sharing is also involved here. The first poem features the name Hari, yielding the twin possibilities of seeing the hero as Krishna (from the perspective of his beloved) or as the supreme deity (from the perspective of a votary, or the individual soul—in other words, everyman). Unlike many other Krishna epithets that allude specifically to some personal characteristic or narrative event, the name Hari encompasses both a broader definition of Vishnu-Krishna and the abstract aspect of God that lies beyond mere narrative and persona; that is to say, its two dimensions allow Hari to sit comfortably with the bhakti representing the deity as respectively "qualified" and "unqualified." Thus we can read the poem as being about the physical presence and absence of Krishna the lover or as alluding to the soul's connectedness to (and woeful awareness of separation from) the divine.

If we apply this background to a reading of the beautifully constructed second poem quoted here, we begin to see that its resonance goes deeper than is commonly acknowledged by the commentators. Most of them propose a simplistic narrative in which a woman dreams of a visit from her lover, then wakes to find the door still locked from within and realizes that it was all "just a dream." This primary meaning is fine as far as it goes, but does it go far enough? Could the words not also suggest an epiphany, an apprehension of a mysterious and ineffable Presence that is felt but not seen?

Bihari's conflation of tropes is the key to his creative character, and a deep vein of wit runs through his compositions. It may occasionally be humorous, but more essentially it reflects an imaginative visionary wisdom that relates to such cognates of "wit" as the Sanskrit words *vidyā, veda*. This is not to imply that every couplet in the *Satsaī* bears some kind of metaphysical profundity, or that a consistent theology (still less some tediously literal allegory) underlies poetic descriptions of female beauty; but a sensitive reading of the *Satsaī* does yield a gift of aesthetic delight that transcends the often conventional contexts of its tropes. Unsurprisingly for a poet in the Braj Bhasha tradition, the needle of Bihari's inner compass swings very naturally to the magnetic north of Krishna devotionalism. But there are also moments of an intense inner quietude that suggest a personal apprehension of divine immanence on a more universal model.

The traditional critical approach to Bihari's poetry derives from the hoary and complex system of rhetoric so famously developed by the Sanskrit masters. Two facets dominate: a standardized typology of characters, narrative settings, and the like; and an elaboration of the so-called "rasa theory," in which individual "flavors" or sentiments (rasa) are borne aloft through art and are hence transformed into a kind of universalized experience of delight that transcends the specific circumstances of the moment. The rasa theory has major ramifications for such fields as philosophy, aesthetics, and devotional theology, and has been developed to a high level of rhetorical sophistication over the centuries.[26] Yet the reader of English translations of Bihari is unlikely to view the poetry through this lens, and the purpose of the present book is to yield some kind of access to the poetry itself. There is much in common between Indic and Western conceptions of the functions of art.[27] Both traditions recognize that the higher reaches of aesthetic experience have a sublime or spiritual dimension in which distinctions between the sacred and the profane lose their relevance. The experience of rasa, triggered by aesthetic stimuli, transcends the details of mere narrative and bears the reader to a higher plane; thus the question of whether or not a poem's dramatis personae and motifs derive from a bhakti setting becomes secondary to the artistic function of the poetic medium.

The *Satsaī* bears witness to Biharilal as a creative individual of profound ingenuity and delightful wit; he brings an immediacy of experience to many a conventional image, and in so doing he reaches to us across time, allowing us direct entry to his poetic world. Though much can be said as commentary to this or that verse (and the notes to this book aim to cast light on certain allusions), the poems themselves stand up remarkably well nearly four centuries after their composition. Unsurprisingly, some work better than others in translation, and this book selects four hundred of the total 717: four centuries of poems, then, from nearly four centuries ago.

Verse Structure and the Translation

Bihari's poems are rhymed couplets written in the *dohā* meter and in a variant called *sorṭhā*. The *dohā* is a favorite meter in the Hindi tradition, found for example in genres of bhakti poetry such as the so-called *sākhīs*, or "witness poems," of Kabir[28] and in the couplets that punctuate sequences of quatrains in the great *Rāmcaritmānas* of Tulsidas.[29] Each line of the *dohā* is divided rhythmically by a caesura that falls just after the midway point—with 13 metrical beats before and 11 after the caesura—effectively dividing the couplet into four quarters or feet. The *sorṭhā* inverts this arrangement, placing the short foot before the long one, with the rhyme now falling at the caesura instead of at the end of the line; *sorṭhā* meter appears in verses 103, 138, 145, 209, 270, 323, and 329.

Since the whole of the *Satsaī* is couched in the *dohā/sorṭhā* meter, a single English format is needed to maintain some structural unity throughout the corpus without proving too much of a metrical straitjacket. A couplet is too short and a quatrain too long; therefore, I settle upon the tercet—definable only by its three lines, not by any set metrical weight or rhyme scheme—as a viable compromise.

I welcome English rhymes when they appear serendipitously, but rhyme's function of bestowing an organic unity to the verse is more often performed by internal rhyme and alliteration—features that abound in the original—than by end rhyme. The second line of the tercet often hinges on a syntactic caesura, as though that line were a compressed form of two separate lines, but elsewhere no such caesura exists. Thus the desired unity of form running throughout my translation is quite loose, consisting simply in the disposition of three lines.

I have tried to emulate the character of the originals through a process of substitution. Since one-to-one replications of Braj puns (and other rhetorical devices) with English equivalents are largely impossible, the desideratum of "faithfulness" has to be met in terms of overall tone rather than detailed specifics. Punning allusions such as "matchless fire" (verse 27), "he truly lives who's dyed in Ram" (verse 91), and "[a knot that's] bound to yield" (verse 325) are substitutes for similar kinds of wordplay somewhere in the originals, but are themselves inventions in the target language. Variations on this technique, used equally with alliteration and rhythm, are applied throughout the translation. My focus has been on the actual moment of each poem; I have tried to suggest the inner stillness at the heart of Bihari's literary art, for his literary wit is at once light and profound.

Many aspects of the couplets, especially playfulness,

structure, and allusions, are explained in the formal analysis offered by the notes.

Acknowledgments

The *Satsaī* has held me in its spell since I first encountered the text through Simon Weightman's Hindi classes at the School of Oriental and African Studies in 1973, and the long intention to translate some part of it has finally borne fruit at the other end of my career, after retirement. My greatest debt of gratitude is to Sheldon Pollock, kindliest and most supportive of editors; through him alone I have the honor of contributing to the illustrious MCLI series. I have also benefited greatly from the wise advice of David Shulman, Francesca Orsini, and Eliot Weinberger at MCLI. Heather Hughes, Emily Silk, and Leslie Kriesel at MCLI have enhanced my text through their insightful editing. Many others have helped me along the way, whether with practical assistance, scholarly counsel, or more general encouragement and chiding, and I give heartfelt thanks to Marina Chellini, Rohini Chowdhury, Gopal Gandhi, Sophie Hartman, Jack Hawley, Akbar Hyder, Aruna Kharod, Janice Leoshko, Renuka Madan, Lakshmidhar Malaviya, Arvind Krishna Mehrotra, Ramkumari Mishra, the late Kunwar Narain, Patrick Olivelle, Shilpa Parnami, Bhavani Parpia, Mary Rader, Andrew Topsfield, the late Rima Treon, and Harish Trivedi.

This translation is dedicated to Renuka, with whom Biharilal himself seems also to have been well acquainted.

NOTES

1 McGregor 1984: 173.
2 Jagannathdas "Ratnakar" 1953: 314–382.
3 The text was allegedly copied by a Hindi scholar named Pandit Harprasad Caturvedi from a manuscript carried by a gentleman encountered on a train journey, and was eventually published in the *Nāgarīpracāriṇī Sabhā Patrikā* (Journal of the Association for the Promotion of Nagari) in 1919.
4 Had Bihari been as much of a musician as is here (and commonly) made out, his text might have been expected to be richer in musical reference.
5 The first true autobiography in Braj Bhasha—perhaps in any Indian language—is the *Ardhakathānaka* (Half a Tale) of Banarasidas, dated V.S. 1698 (1641 C.E.); see Chowdhury 2009 and Snell 2005.
6 Jagannathdas "Ratnakar" 1953: 321. Employing one of the standard methodologies of such historical sleuthing, Ratnakar points out a mismatch between the days of the week and lunar dates specified in the text.
7 For introductions to the language, see Snell 1991 and McGregor 1968; for an overview of its literature see McGregor 1984; and for its courtly traditions see Busch 2011.
8 See Miltner 1961 and Busch 2010.
9 Verse 27.
10 See Khoroche and Tieken 2009 for a discussion of the possible dates of the *Sattasaī* of Hala.
11 Basak 1971: 12.
12 Mehrotra 1991: 5.
13 Verse 82.
14 Verse 386.
15 Verse 197.
16 Verse 14.
17 See Rākeśagupta 1967 and Gerow 1971.
18 Capulet: "She hath not seen the change of fourteen years"—*Romeo and Juliet* 1.II.9.
19 See Snell 1994 for a fuller discussion.
20 Bryant 2003.
21 Jayadeva 1977.
22 See Miltner 1963 for a discussion of Bihari's musicality.

23 Verse 226.

24 Verse 257.

25 The rhyme *kapāṭa/bāṭa* (and its rhetoric) has a precedent in *Rāmcaritmānas, Sundarkāṇḍ* 30. See Tulsidas 2020: 260.

26 Many of the primary texts for rasa theory are presented in Pollock 2016.

27 There are also countless major divergences in the two critical systems. Repetition of a word is regarded as a poetic fault (*punarokti doṣa*) in the Indic tradition, whereas the modern English poet and theorist Glyn Maxwell (2013: 53) can say, "Regarding repetition, there is none in poetry"—meaning that the second occurrence of a word lacks virginity and therefore has a new and different semantic character.

28 See Vaudeville 1974.

29 See Tulsidas 2016–2023.

He Spoke of Love

May Radha the sublime, whose golden glow   1
greens Krishna's raincloud blue,
clear from my path the hindrance of the world.[1]

As breasts, hearts, eyes, and hips   2
hold sway in body politic,
astute king youth gives all a handsome raise.[2]

Eagerly intent, and goaded by the god of love,   3
rushing on in rivalry:
her heart, her wits, her eyes.

The lady merged with moonlight,   4
lost from view; her friends swarmed after,
following a thread of fragrance.[3]

With fearful dread I saw the moon rise in the lane   5
when by a happy circumstance
the bees that thronged around me dimmed its glow.[4]

Her loveliness will thrill you, handsome Lal,   6
as it thrilled me; she gleams so bright it seems
her lily garland's jasmine golden.[5]

Idly sidling, spilling soul's secrets,   7
blind to occasion, ever changing,
luster drunk: these errant eyes.

3

8 You saved a single elephant,
  then quit as savior, so it seems.
  You turn a fine deaf ear to my poor cry.[6]

9 Shame's moorings torn, my heart's sent reeling—
  a wayward craft wheeling
  in the whirlpool of those charms.[7]

10 From deep inside her veil she throws a glance,
  contrives sweet touch of shadows,
  and is gone.[8]

11 As though well schooled by love in yogic lore,
  her eyes reach out to her temples
  in search of union.[9]

12 A visit to her natal home yields joy,
  while distance from her lover leads to grief:
  in balance, like Duryodhana, she dies.[10]

13 Glimmering through fine veil, a matchless glow—
  a budding bough of the tree of paradise
  gleaming, glinting, in ocean's waters.

14 Beauty, that brigand, struck my traveler eyes,
  dazzled them with her body's sheen, noosed them
  with a silken smile, ditched them in the dimple on her
   chin.[11]

A thousand efforts cannot draw it out: 15
like salt in water, Mohan's form
infuses my heart.

The bedded flower shall surely bear its fruit   16
if saved from scorching anger; oh gardener,
just tend your bed with drops of tenderness.

Pān juice on eyes, eye black on lips, foot lac on brow: 17
well met, well done, well come indeed.
Your look becomes you, Lal.[12]

Those smiling eyes—   18
shy and proud, languid yet thrilled;
their dawning luster tells a tale of night-felt joys.

He spoke of love: she smiled, glanced at her friends; 19
and one by one, delightedly,
they made excuses, took their leave.

Though strained on cresting her breast, his gaze   20
strove onward to her face; then tumbled down
chin-dimple dell—and lies there still.

It faces each in turn, then turns away: 21
the needle of a compass is her gaze,
which settles finally on him alone.[13]

22 Speaking, spurning, thrilling, fretting,
    meeting, blooming, blushing—
    in a public place, all is said with eyes alone.

23 You yearn for my rival, and stumble as you walk.
    For all your treachery, your coming here
    cools the yearning that burns my heart.[14]

24 Seeing her in company, Shyam touched a lotus
    to his brow; she caught him in her mirror ring
    and held him to her heart.[15]

25 The barber's wife began to lac the lady's feet;
    thinking it the lac ball,
    she rubbed the lady's heel over and over.[16]

26 No pollen yet, no sweet nectar, no blooming flower;
    the bee's already held within the bud,
    so who can tell what the future may hold?[17]

27 Your absence is a rare and matchless fire:
    it flourishes in monsoon rains.
    No waterfall, oh Lal, can douse its blaze.[18]

28 The more the bride's young body finds its glow
    the more her rivals' faces
    lose their gleam.[19]

As our eyes see all around, but not themselves,   29
so God reveals the world entire
but remains unseen.[20]

He laughs to see her charming mole applied: 30
"How well, face-like-the-moon, you've made
your moon face like the moon."[21]

Confounded by the lady's heels,   31
already madder red, she wonders,
"Who would redden such a foot?"[22]

Bathed in pools of love,   32
these eyes put lilies in the shade;
though lacking kohl, they darken the wagtail's name.

How strange the fire of loneliness that's kindled   33
in her heart: inflamed by rosewater,
tamed by a lover's gusts of endearments.

Hiding in the dark wood of your blue sari,   34
they don't miss their prey: your cheetah eyes
never fail to seize my deerlike heart.[23]

No one can know my loving heart—   35
the deeper it is steeped in Shyam's dark shade,
the brighter shines its glow.

36 Ah yes! Unveil your face,
     that all may feast their eyes:
     let the lotus weep, may the moon be mocked.[24]

37 Pining for your company, dear Lal,
     she sees the blazing volcano of love
     and consigns all happy comfort to the flames.

38 It doesn't matter if we're apart—our hearts are joined:
     whichever way a kite may fly,
     its string lies in the flyer's hand.[25]

39 Paper won't carry it, nor do I dare say it:
     your heart alone will bear
     the burden of mine.

40 What wretch did you befriend,
     whom did you ever save, oh savior Raghurai?
     You strut about self-satisfied, so falsely famed.[26]

41 My husband's forsaken all memory of me;
     to whom shall I call, who will hear?
     The wayward monsoon clouds thunder in rivalry.[27]

42 I'd thought our meeting eyes would doubly glow;
     who knew your gaze would rankle
     like a mote in mine?

She drew him close in passion's grip,   43
but then her words remained half said:
her lover's shame-filled eyes filled hers with rage.

I told you many times, don't trust those eyes.   44
They soon collide, collude,
ignite the heart.

The time is gone, Kanha, when just a little virtue   45
earned your grace; now even you are giving
at the going rate.[28]

For years I've cried my rote, but Shyam, you pay no heed; 46
"World Guru, Lord of the World," you too
feel the winds of the world.

Jewels glimmer on every limb of her flamelike frame; 47
douse the lamp, and even then the house will shine
as bright as day.

Her youthful luster grows, yet a childish glint   48
still glows; she shines with mingled brilliance
of shot-silk twines entwined.[29]

Don't be afraid, dear Shyam, of fuming words: 49
her doting dancing eyes bespeak
an ardent heart.

50 You'll need an almanac around that house:
    her lustrous face glows constantly
    with full moon's gleam.[30]

51 Bathed, she lingers, dresses her hair;
    through fingers and long black strands
    her flighty wagtail eyes spy Nandkumar.[31]

52 Your brow is smeared with lac—it sears my eyes like fire:
    you'll fast deny it, Lal,
    but will the glass belie it?[32]

53 In face of Jai Shah, lakhs are bettered in battle;
    and even the unlettered bear off lakhs
    in bounty for the asking.[33]

54 Your gift to me is mine, dwells with my soul;
    do not lay that heart, my love,
    in rival hands.

55 Let others hoard a million, store trillions away;
    my wealth is ever Jadupati,
    who dispels adversity.

56 Scripture's path's untrod, and the world's afraid:
    for on the lofty summit of her breasts
    the tribesman Kamdev takes a stand.[34]

A raised hand veils her head, reveals her navel folds— 57
then down the lane she goes, screened by her friend,
holding my eyes with a steady glance.

Laughingly, you gifted it that distant day, 58
and even now, your berry garland
saves her volatile camphor soul.[35]

Fair skin, ripening breasts, yellow mark on brow; 59
with flighty eyes and haughty pose
the village beauty strikes me down.[36]

A singing lyre, verse elixir, sweet melody 60
of love: they are lost who do not drown
in these, yet saved are they who drown for good.[37]

Simply sleek, darkly bright, fragrantly soft— 61
my heart knows no right path or wrong
on seeing her hair in disarray arrayed.

The vine of love is not burned at all 62
in the fiery blaze of loneliness: it grows
full green and thrusts and thrives.

Forgo this smiling guise a while: 63
these shining teeth so dazzle me
your face lies hidden in the glow.

64 A crocodile pendant gleams at Gopal's ear:
Kamdev has pitched camp within his heart, it seems,
and leaves his pennant glinting at the door.[38]

65 A tremulous earring glimmers through her white veil
like the reflection of the sun at dawn
shimmering on Ganga's waters.[39]

66 With seething brow and cold harsh words
I strive in vain to numb my heart; a glimpse
of Hari fills my eyes with smiles again.

67 Next to her youthful body's shadow,
the moonlight itself a mere shadow seems.
Which young girl's luster now will please the eye?

68 Like summer days, the young girl's breasts
fill out and grow; just so her waist, like summer nights,
attenuates.[40]

69 Wasted by love's pain, she's barely seen;
like a guttering flame, Hari, she cries out
when she hears your name.[41]

70 Red skies have banished night, birds sounded dawn:
Krishna, wreathed in forest flowers, tends love elsewhere,
my friend, and has not come.

In slumbering dreams, 71
Shyamghan lingers with me, dispels my loneliness;
but sleep slips silently away—and earns my curse.

Deeds of the great won't thrive through little men. 72
Tell me, can a mouse skin
cover a kettledrum?[42]

"Like lotuses," poets declare; but I'd say eyes are stone; 73
what else could spark this lovesick fire
when hers strike mine?

Hari, Hari! She burns and burns. 74
I'm done with cures. I swear, good doctor;
your tonic alone can bring her fever down.

Lal gave it from his breast before her rivals' eyes; 75
she blooms with pleasure as she goes about
with that crumpled garland.[43]

Newly in love, the lady has her comely lover's ring— 76
admires it, kisses it, holds it close, wears it,
takes it off, and stores it away.

The tender swan of her soul still lives! 77
Thus we infer that stooping death hawks
fear the flames of separation's fire.

78   Ward off the sun a while in a grove by the Yamuna;
     fair jasmine entwines the dark *tamāl* tree—
     ease-giving riverbank, loud with bees.[44]

79   He laughed and urged his to a halt,
     she gave him hers and smiled a smile:
     eyes met, hearts met, as they merged their herds.[45]

80   He's on his back, and she's astride him.
     Her waist bells sing a fanfare
     and her anklets hold their tongue.[46]

81   He touched her foot, that she might come on top;
     she smiled, said not a word, put out the lamp,
     and so gave her reply.[47]

82   Settling within the dense wood,
     lurking deep within the house: at summer's noon,
     even shadow seeks shade.[48]

83   Your heated words
     won't stop me savoring their taste—
     like simmered milk, sweeter by the second.

84   Who'd ever find her in the wild,
     hidden among fair jasmine,
     if her own bouquet didn't betray her?[49]

The cane is dug, the cotton gone, the flax all dried;   85
but green, green stands the lentil field—
so cleave to your courage, my girl.[50]

With faltering steps she walks away,   86
pauses, glances, looks, and leaves;
this lovely lady, thief of hearts, makes off with mine.

If you'd observe her body's state,   87
then go by all means, sir, and take a look—
but quietly and without delay.

At the door she turned, glanced artfully, and smiled;   88
she'd come for curd to turn the milk,
but as she left she turned my heart.

Though a moment's ride on a steady horse,   89
the path from village boundaries to her house became
a thousand leagues.[51]

Hearing from her friends one winter day   90
"Your husband is set to leave," the artful lady
took her lute and played a monsoon melody.[52]

Rosaries and pious show all count for naught,   91
and the false mind dances brazenly in vain;
he truly lives who's dyed in Ram.

92   Heading to the wood, he comes this way,
     aglow with laughing smiles; with bird-lime glance
     he's snared my wagtail eyes.[53]

93   Humbly he tramps from house to house,
     begging from one and all; through the lens of greed,
     even the small are magnified.

94   Wherever that capricious bather takes the plunge
     she lends the waters there
     a saffron tinge.[54]

95   His hands jet water into his young bride's eyes,
     reddening the corners
     of the eyes of her rivals.[55]

96   What have your feisty eyes done now?
     Lal falls distraught: here lies his little flute,
     his yellow sash; here his garland, there his crown.

97   With Radha dressed as Hari, he as she,
     they trade roles in their woodland tryst.
     So who's above? The lover or his love?

98   Both good and bad win riches, rubies, gems,
     and strings of pearls: fortune marks the brow of those
     gifted with the presence of Jai Shah.

They'll see neither fame nor infamy,   99
they see only his dusky form. What can I do?
These hasty, greedy eyes run wherever they will.

Though brimful with his lovely limbs, they crave a smile: 100
my greedy eyes will not forsake
their yearning.

You touch her little finger, then her wrist—   101
and with such humble show. But none will trust you
who know the tale of Bali and the dwarf.[56]

Behold the mystery of Shyam's enchanting form— 102
dwelling within the heart, and yet
reflected throughout the world.[57]

This I have found for sure: 103
the world's a blemished glass—
a single boundless form is seen reflected there.[58]

Roaming down the rolling road   104
I met a prancing dancer all aglow
with gleaming crown.[59]

Ardently scribed by a lover's zestful heart,   105
the note—a knife to lovesick pain—
lies hard against her chest.[60]

106 Enviously her friends admire, dear Lal, her
lively girlish charms: of late her breasts reveal
some growing trends.

107 Seeing the lady's tearful eyes,
the lover lingers, will not leave; his voice falters;
haltingly, he holds her to his heart.

108 Jai Shah's reflected glory shines in the mirrored hall
as though the god of love had massed a corps
to conquer the world.[61]

109 "My girl, what is this blush in the corner
of your eyes?" "Why Lal, it's nothing
but the flush of yours in mine."[62]

110 Leaving me, he bears my joys away;
to summer days and winter nights
his parting gives long leases on my heart.[63]

111 It comes and goes unnoticed, all's gone cold;
like a son-in-law who's always in the house,
the winter day soon forfeits novel favor.[64]

112 By force these eyes embezzle the heart's rich funds:
highway robbers even to the cautious,
thieves even to the watchful.

Come, friend. As cowherds leave their meeting place   113
and dust from homebound cow hooves dims the path,
it's time for evening's amble to the tryst.[65]

Firm heroes in the field, they find their mark: 114
a throng of thousands won't impede
these willful eyes.

Merry with wine, the young lady laughs   115
and looks at him; bubbling, babbling,
she craves him so, entwines him.

On brow so fair her sandal *bindī* lies concealed,   116
but as the wine flushes her face,
so will it stand revealed.[66]

Shyam, charm's diadem: 117
wherever once they saw him stand
my eyes are held awhile—though he's not there.

Steeped in joy   118
from a sleepless night in lover's arms,
she falters as she walks, stretching, preening.

Like a digit of the moon in an emerald water bowl,   119
a nail mark on your dusky skin
gleams through your gossamer gown.[67]

120   Due to bed a rival, he revels with a third;
      so all at once our lady's glad and sad,
      wrathful and relishing, riled and smiling.[68]

121   Her bosom lies barely concealed
      by bodice and moist white sari; like the
      thrust of a poet's figures, evident to all.[69]

122   Words fail the blended grace of form and clothing:
      her bodice clad in body's glow,
      not vice versa.[70]

123   Between the rooftops
      two hearts prance along a rope of glances:
      fearlessly, like acrobats, this way and that they go.[71]

124   Greedy for Hari's assets, my ignoble eyes
      struck a secret deal with him, and
      sold me off right there and then.

125   Up she slides, slick and sleek,
      subtle, supple as a cane: serpentine,
      the swarthy savory lady bites and slips away.[72]

126   Their glances clashed, engaged—
      her veil too weak a vanguard to impede
      his eyes as they fell on her company.[73]

They're saffron stamens, clinging to his skin: 127
how naughty to imply
they're nail marks.

Forgoing pilgrimage, cherish the radiance 128
of Hari and Radha: the pleasure groves of Braj
become Prayag at every step along the lane.[74]

Constantly this chafes my mind: 129
as she slipped through the crowd without a glance,
what were those words that passed her lips?

A proper tone eludes as yet 130
this body, wasted by love's loneliness.
Can talk of leaving start so soon?[75]

With his own hand Lal wove it and laid it on her breast, 131
where the pale medlar garland
gained new grace.

With new love playing in her heart, yet shy at home, 132
she flutters to and fro, a shuttle in a loom.
So her days pass.

From here to there, and back again, 133
no peace or pause; she's restless as a spinning top,
by turns she comes and goes.

134 She leaves for her lover's house
  clad in a blue mantle and the dark of night.
  How can this guise disguise her glow?

135 From loveliness alone, it seems,
  the love god as creator shaped these thighs—
  painful to plantain trees, a joy to young lovers.[76]

136 Wrath in her frown and mind and eyes, she grips the bed:
  she'd dreamed he was untrue to her—
  and now awake, her heart's withdrawn.

137 However bold, however many times they try,
  how can my eyes cross the salty sea
  of that body's loveliness?

138 Grant me salvation, as you do to many poor souls;
  but if bonds find your favor,
  bind me in the strands of your being.

139 That tyrant youth snatched a girl's body as his realm,
  turned small to great and great to small,
  switched everything about.[77]

140 Her fluttering eye and leaping heart and radiant limbs:
  her lover not yet come, the doe-eyed lady
  thrills as she puts on her finery.[78]

Delayed in doorway greetings,   141
the entrance of my beloved, lord of my life,
takes not a moment but an age.[79]

Am I mad with love's pain, or is the whole world mad?   142
What were they thinking when
they named the moon "cool-rayed"?[80]

Asleep, awake, dreaming, joyful, angry,   143
quiet, or restless, my mind can never forgo
memories of loving cloud-dark Shyam.

You count yourself so great, grand *gopīs'* lord.   144
So shall I too call you when you see her hands
and keep your heart in hand.[81]

She sits, face veiled, contemplative: 145
anchorite eyes enchained with lashes,
strings of cowrie shells as tears.[82]

Heed well in your heart: 146
the moon is risen this autumn night
as Kamdev's royal canopy overspreads the earth.[83]

No moonlight, this. A pall of darkness   147
makes the world its home, yet pales
in fear of the rising moon.[84]

148   When wealth declines, we take it as mere fate;
to think the same in affluence
would speed us to salvation's gate.

149   Forever one in manner, mind, and tender age:
a proper vision of the youthful pair requires
a thousand pairs of eyes.[85]

150   Wise to yourself, you disregard my words;
but when love strikes, don't lay your soul too soon
in alien hands.[86]

151   Hari, a thousand times I pray:
whatever my fate may be, let me lodge forever
in a corner of your court.[87]

152   Your languid limbs gleam with new nail marks,
your eyes will not meet mine:
why protest your innocence?

153   Even in the cool summerhouse,
where noontime fire becomes a winter's night,
she writhes, she burns.[88]

154   The curd pot set aside, with stirring stick upside down,
she stirs but water in the turning jar,
this novice churning girl.

Her skin flared up where flowers fell   155
from her husband's brother's hand; she laughed
as friends, confused, tended these welts.[89]

Glances for lances, eyelids as shields,   156
with many a feint their lusty eyes
thrust and parry a thousand strikes.

Daisy chain adorns her breast, straw pendant her brow: 157
the country girl with outstanding bosom
stands out watching the field.[90]

As though forswearing any sound   158
except the flute's, she trains her ear
toward the forest, night and day.[91]

"Don't assume you are free, with your cheating heart."   159
"If you hold me guilty, then hold me
tightly captive in your eyes."

Its depths would drown a thousand ardent hearts   160
high as mountains; yet it's ankle-deep,
this sea of love, to brutes of men.

They're filling out, some tender weight is on its way.   161
Pretending to admire her necklace shells,
she sizes up her budding breasts through night and day.

162 Limb brushes limb
in a dark and narrow lane—
a well-known touch, well known again.[92]

163 Blossom time is over, spring has passed.
Poor bee, my friend, the rosebush leaves
a leafless, thorny branch.[93]

164 So many times I tell you this:
don't turn, lie still—lest rosy petals
graze your limbs.

165 Steeply stoops her hawkish gaze;
then, soaring, grabs the heron of my heart,
shakes it savagely, brings it down.[94]

166 I yearn, but cannot tend my neighbor love,
whose sighs, screened by this trellis,
rend my heart.

167 His text was on adultery.
She glanced at him and beamed;
the erudite reciter smothered a smile.[95]

168 Lovingly, nervously, joyfully, trembling,
perspiring, smiling, she took my soul in hand
and placed a *pān* in mine.

"Like looks well with like"—so say they all: 169
red lips are the place for *pān* stains,
dark eyes for kohl.[96]

My soul counts for nothing, friend,   170
its being and nonbeing are as one; let it lie
in my body like a nonday in the almanac.[97]

Urbanity? They clap and mock the very word;   171
going to the village, every shred
of pride and virtue's gone for good.

He looked at her, threw playful Holi powder   172
in her eyes; and though it smarts, she cannot bear
to wipe the pain away.

Covered in damp clothing,   173
and that too on a winter's night,
from love alone her companions dare approach her.[98]

I've heated heart's hammam with triple fires,   174
that passing Shyam might linger, tingle,
warm toward me, melt a while.[99]

That master, love, has trained them well.   175
Like dancing pupils are the pupils of her eyes
that leap and dart with boundless grace.

176 A traveler from her village tells of summer winds
on winter nights. What's left to ask or say? We know
for sure, the lovesick lady's still alive.

177 Her rival's lac-red feet were quite enough to bear
till her lover's red-stained fingers
ignited a more furious fire.[100]

178 Lovingly at the lifting of the bridal veil,
mother-in-law yielded the house,
husband his heart, rival wives their happiness.[101]

179 Why hesitate? Roam where you will—
you're not at fault. No matter if your winsome eyes
should win some hearts.

180 Recalling loving Shyam, Radhika stares
at the Yamuna shore; and for a spell, she salts
the bankside waters with her tears.[102]

181 Swollen with *gopīs'* tears, undrying, shoreless,
the rising river runs through every lane,
through every house and every door.

182 Lost in thought, she does not move or waver, smile
or fret: staring at her lover staring at a picture—
a very picture she.

Noticing her small and dainty hands, 183
her father-in-law made her the giver of alms; but
craving her charms, all the world comes to the door.[103]

As the new bride sheds all trace of childishness, 184
to her rival wives the husband seems as dear
as if he left for foreign lands.

You quite enshrine the lovely form of Harihara— 185
a fingernail's fine crescent on your brow,
a goddess in your heart.[104]

She won't let heal the swelling welt 186
of a nail mark left at her lover's leaving:
over and over, she picks at the scratch.[105]

With crowned head and girdled waist, 187
with flute in hand and garland on your chest:
in such a guise dwell ever in my heart, Biharilal.[106]

With flirting brow and flashing yellow sash, 188
with swaying walk and glinting gaze,
Biharilal has stolen my heart.

The grove lies deep in blackest night, 189
yet, dusky Shyam, she's not concealed—
like a radiant flame she makes her way.

190   "Bad company leads all astray"—it's truly said.
From brows so arched and raked derives
her arch and rakish glance.[107]

191   See how a border of golden thread
frames the gleam of this lovely face,
as lightning haloes the autumn moon.

192   A glance of guileless ease, a fair-faced smile,
an arm flung round her bosom friend—
how she disturbs my mind.[108]

193   Plunging into Hari's liquid grace, there's no release:
like pails on a Persian wheel, over and over
my eyes fill, flow, dive, and rise again.

194   As for tactics, parley's failed, dissent is spent.
So lay a mine of love and seize the denizen
of high-walled Fort Intransigence.

195   My friend, the berry garland glows so bright
on Gopal's breast, you'd think the forest fire he drank
burned from within.[109]

196   Don't let your momentary married bliss
go to your head; for summer's shade
is no one's friend in winter's cold.[110]

On the festival of Teej, her rivals dressed in finery   197
and gems; but how their faces crumpled when they saw
her rumpled clothes.[111]

Bows, brows, bastions, lashes, locks, and glances,   198
each one's enhanced by obliquity—
and a girl, and a horse, and a catch of melody.[112]

Six or seven cubits, to and fro she flies   199
as though she rode a swing
propelled by sighs.[113]

The brazen lover spoke of making love with her on top;   200
she looked at him askance,
while coyness, anger, rapture lit her eyes.

She drew me with a glance, then veiled herself   201
in languor; my doting eyes stood on tiptoe
to see again that doe-eyed girl.

How will her tender frame sustain   202
the weight of ornament? Burdened by splendor alone,
her foot falls faltering upon the floor.[114]

Sweetness on lips, eyes oozing love, eyebrows at ease—   203
but it's your constant deference that
disturbs my heart.

204   Although her lips reiterate a constant "No sir, no!"
      she smiles with rakish eyebrow—ah,
      she's miles from meaning so.

205   A moment's visit and you'll never get away.
      In the city of love, the stricken are struck at every turn
      and the killer prowls at his pleasure.

206   The starry sky of her mantle enfolds
      a moonlight face, and love bears down like sleep
      as I behold my Lady Night.

207   A little "o," the world agrees, augments tenfold;
      but painted on a woman's brow
      it brightens beyond all telling.[115]

208   It's burnt below, and
      stained above with kohl-black tears:
      he reads her note's unwritten lovesick tale.[116]

209   Absence withers her, but nourishes her love—
      as rain will waste the thornbush,
      but feed the rose.[117]

210   On golden limbs her gold's unseen;
      by touch alone—harsh to the hand—
      her jewelry is known.[118]

Dulling her luster, 211
lessening her radiance:
the balm on her limbs is like breath on a glass.[119]

Wear no ornaments of gold. 212
And here is why: they seem like rust
that stains the mirror of your skin.

No matter if she's out of sorts, young loving man, 213
this girl is always pure delight: even
the hardest knot in sugarcane is sugar sweet.

Clad in fine white, she's at her loveliest; 214
her body's gleam is like a lamp
behind a waterfall's cascade.[120]

Eyes fixed on the wintry sun, 215
the partridge thinks it a January moon,
delighting in night's coolness at the height of day.

Warming sun, raging fire, thickest of quilts— 216
nothing conquers winter's chill
till a woman's limbs cling to her man's.

Quitting the world for fear of winter cold, 217
warmth flees to the safe mountain refuge
of a woman's breasts.[121]

218   Knowing them false, the heart
     sets little store by spoken words:
     that's why the Lord made eyes for talking.

219   So many master artists, puffed up with pride,
     begin to paint her likeness
     and lose their way.

220   Turning away, glancing back,
     lifting the edge of her veil, casting
     a fistful of *gulāl*,[122] she casts her spell.

221   As red *gulāl* flies from her hand,
     both shyness and decorum fly away, and
     lovers' hearts and eyes at once are tinged.

222   The more my lady, a lapping flame,
     wraps me to her breast, the more my heart is cooled
     as though soothed by rosewater.

223   Where did you study archery, my love?
     Your brows are a bow without a string, yet your
     darting glances never miss the flighty heart.

224   Her eyelids glisten with tears, for she's just heard
     he's soon to leave; an artful yawn conceals the cause
     even from her friends.

Blending in tone with the golden girl,   225
the camphor balm that limns her limbs
is known by scent alone.

How shall Hari gain the chamber of my heart   226
while falsehood's latch and bolt
lock tight the door?[123]

Her stringed pearls, blending with her body's brilliance,   227
turn amber colored. Even her canny friend
tests them with a straw.[124]

The courtyard lady spies her lover's kite   228
and flies about like one entranced,
touching its dancing shadow.[125]

All praise, no doubt, the tumbler pigeons' flight.   229
But the gleam in your eye, the bloom in your face,
your trembling form—what's this about?[126]

Steeped in love's essence,   230
her heart melts in the flames of separation
and drips as teardrops from her eyes.[127]

There's but one way to cross this worldly sea: 231
embark on the boat of Hari's name
and make a rudder of your rosary.[128]

232   Now shining forth, now shrinking back,
       arm round his neck: girl on a rooftop,
       cloud-gazing, lightning bright.[129]

233   To take the child from my arms, the trickster's game:
       he came up close and brushed a finger on my breast,
       and in a heartbeat was gone again.

234   She talks and laughs as one beyond her years;
       his eyes, carousing, never leave
       his tipsy young bride.

235   With bees for bells, oozing the nectar of flowers,
       gently, gently through the grove
       strolls the elephant breeze.[130]

236   Dripping nectar, lingering under the trees,
       wearily ambling as it comes—
       the southerly breeze.

237   Clad in flower pollen, drenched in nectar—
       like a young bride comes the lovely breeze
       gently bearing joy.

238   "No fault, no fear," the saying goes.
       Why then this needless shame?
       If your word is true, then meet my gaze.[131]

Lest it be soiled or lose its shine, my friend,   239
save your loving heart
from lusty passion's dust.

Try as you might, you cannot hide your love;   240
a novel dryness in your eyes
bespeaks a melting heart.

Lal, what kind of beauty is this?   241
A moment's sight of you denies the eye
a moment's closing.

The arch of love requires at first a go-between's support;   242
once built, it's at its best
with framework all removed.[132]

She neither speaks with a smile nor glances   243
with dancing eyes; a growing coldness in her face
bespeaks a growing ardor.

Perfectly preserved on your white sleeve: 244
an impress of the braid
of a tightly cleaving, doe-eyed maid.

This is no time for other means: 245
seek out that boatman
who crossed the ocean on a boat of stone.[133]

246   The shy young bride strays,
       swayed by wine: the more brazen,
       the sweeter she becomes.

247   Listless with longing, his eyes won't leave
       the flushed face of the young girl—
       beaded with sweat, tired from woodland games.

248   Hari holds the tender lotus lady in his heart,
       shunning sandalwood, garland, and balm
       lest they weigh her down within.[134]

249   How could one live, and how survive
       in the lawless town of love? Eyes assail
       freely, while innocent hearts are bound.

250   Be it shallow or deep,
       river, well, pool, or lake
       is an ocean to him whose thirst it slakes.

251   Feigned anger on her brow, vexed words on her lips:
       she dares not lift her gaze, lest he should see
       her sweetly smiling eyes.

252   As though to save her body's perfect glow
       God made a doormat of her gems—
       for roving eyes to wipe their feet.[135]

Your face fakes coldness,   253
your mouth, dry frosty words:
but how to chill these warm and loving eyes?[136]

The more they drink their fill,   254
the more they thirst: his savory form
can never slake my yearning eyes.

The glow of lips and eyes and sash shines   255
on the greenwood flute in Hari's hands
with rainbow tinge.[137]

Her lover's playful hand covered her eyes; while 256
knowing all, she made as if she did not know
that gentle touch.

Awakening, I see the door still chained.   257
So who can say how he comes in
and vanishes again?[138]

As I have been, so shall I remain, Hari,   258
in my own way; the task is just too hard,
Gopal, do not insist on saving me.[139]

Let the world reprove, I'll not renounce my wayward ways; 259
you'd suffer dwelling in a straightened heart,
Lal, with your three curves.[140]

260   Unreel the string, and God, like a kite, flies far away;
      unbound by yarn,
      he lies here close at hand.[141]

261   Scripture and law books say, and the wise agree:
      oppressors of the weak are three—
      kings, sickness, sins.

262   Who can reprove the great, however great
      their flaws? None but the almighty gave
      the thorny rose those blossoms.[142]

263   No one is well or badly formed—
      a moment comes for all to find beauty;
      as heart's taste deems, so its object appeals.

264   Who can traverse the ocean of this world
      when woman's beauty, lurking in the deep,
      leaps up to seize one's passing shade?[143]

265   With this one hope the bee attends the withered rose:
      that spring will come again to give
      these thorny stems those blossoms.[144]

266   No courtly gallants here to praise your fame;
      in the vulgar village, rose, your blooming
      or nonblooming is all the same.

Let us be off! Who'd trade in elephants 267
in such a town? What do they know,
these potters, diggers, washermen?[145]

Pān juice shines through her limpid neck— 268
a radiant line
as red as a necklace of rubies.[146]

A straying lock of curly hair 269
augments the splendor of her face
as a crescent tells a rupee from a *dām*.[147]

As though the pain of parting brought rain and lightning, 270
my eyes both weep and burn
through all the watches of the night and day.

Why ply your clever moves in vain? 271
A stringless garland
strings out your virtues' yarn across your heart.[148]

Your full breasts' weight, heavy with the freight 272
of budding youth, burdens your rivals' hearts:
they breathe in gasps.[149]

That same approach, that same combing touch— 273
what can explain it? He who entangled my heart
is he who untangled my hair.

274   Love's etching on the paper of the heart
      lay quite unseen; but warmed by lovesick pain, it shows
      like writing in milk-bush sap.[150]

275   Though talk is rife in every house, she will not
      stay long at home; mindfully, unmindfully,
      it's to his door she wends her way.

276   Her husband disrobes her, bent on love,
      but even in the candlelight she's unashamed—
      from head to foot she's wrapped in beauty's glow.

277   Her lover's hand dashed forward to lay her bare,
      but her eyes gave modesty a hideaway
      deep in a thicket of lashes.

278   As love began, shy shyness left for shame;
      then sliding sidelong, sidling close,
      bold boldness came.[151]

279   Shrinking shyly from her lover, smiling, stretching,
      she veiled herself a little, turned away,
      and yawned.[152]

280   One fellow's drenched, one's mired in mud,
      a thousand borne away; what heinous deeds
      the flooding stream of youth wreaks in the world.

Her very blows appease me 281
and her insults too are sweet:
so too, her ardent anger lacks no smile.

Suddenly, a peacock in the woods 282
starts dancing out of season: I know for sure
that Nanda's boy has gladdened this place.

With groves and woods in flower all round, 283
it seems that spring, king of seasons,
had made an arrow cage for parted lovers.[153]

Her golden body gleams in a white sari: 284
lightning in the autumn cloud
has lost its luster, Lal.

For fear that a finger's touch might bruise 285
such tender feet, with trembling heart
they're pumiced with a rose.

Even sages pine for women, 286
their eyes awash with love,
when rainclouds stoop and touch the earth.

In deep monsoon darkness 287
none can tell night from day, but for
the calling of the sheldrake and his mate.[154]

288   The brutish clouds have all dispersed, and all the roads
are running clear; the kingly hero of the autumn sun
has come and set the world at ease.

289   Red lotus hands and feet, eyes wagtail tremulous
and face moon bright. Who'd fail to feel
the timely charms of autumn?

290   These are not fiery June winds blowing,
but rather summer's sighs
as springtime leaves.[155]

291   Don't set her in your heart as Hari would,
nor sit her side-by-side as Hara might,
but hold her tight as tight, and limb to limb.[156]

292   Gorged on mango fragrance, sated
with jasmine scent, honey-drunk
bees bumble about, dazed and drowsy.

293   With your eyelids reddened by lips
and your words and vows so treacherous,
how dare you raise your languid gaze to mine?

294   Oh lovely boy,
until she deigns to speak to you a while
you'll ever yearn for nectar, liquor, sugarcane.

Standing on tiptoe, elbows propped on the wall,   295
peeking round with rolling eyes, each
sweetly kissed the other's cheeks.

A loving night's festivities?   296
Those half-closed smiling eyes
testify to nightlong joys.

The very word "postponement" hits her hard;   297
and what is worse, the sight of mango blossoms
drives her mad.

Don't talk of flowers, or moonlight's glow,   298
or how brightly a mirror can shine.
Just see this lady's luster and your eyes will gleam.

Lying on her fair neck,   299
her white jasmine garland bears a glow
as though the very touch brought ecstasy.

Though steeped in passion, they're still   300
not done; their love-charged eyes
have volleys of beauty yet to fire.

Why does that fearsome dark one come to the house?   301
I've often seen you tremble
at the sight of him.

302 She withers in lovesickness
like a manhandled flower; even
her closest friends barely know her.

303 It's such a time
when even pleasing things give pain; the radiance
of this springtime moon will strike me down.[157]

304 Why fabricate such hurtful lies?
Your words ring hollow when I see
this line of lac upon your brow.

305 Smiling shyly as she speaks,
the fair girl makes me long to hear
her artless talk, her tiny shynesses.

306 Today a novel look shines in your eyes;
feistily it tells a tale
of loving hearts.

307 Composure gone, she flies this way and
that and back again, like one aflame,
in deepening pain all night and day.

308 Drawn equally by shyness and desire,
she has no rest: she peeps on tiptoe,
hides, and peeps—and, hiding, peeps again.

Limbs youthful, supple, lithe as a tendril;   309
her waist, a limber wand,
delights my eyes.

Motionless, a picture on a page,   310
heedless of worldly shame,
she stares at—tell me—whom?

Who does not weep   311
when her parrot intones the pained lament
of this lonesome beloved?

Veiled, her lovely face gleams   312
beneath a blue veil; like a moon it seems,
glimmering in Yamuna's water.

Helpless with wine, she makes play with her fury—   313
fuming and laughing, laughing and fuming,
she fumes and laughs.

In pain she sends her wordless letter;   314
in solitude, attentively
he reads the empty page.

Whipped on by love, flighty with desire,   315
tossing restively, reined in by shyness,
her eyes paw the ground.

316   As night draws near, impatience soars
      and longing grows; dancing, prancing,
      she does her household chores.

317   All clamor for their favored creeds,
      yet every way of worship leads to one alone—
      to Nanda's boy.

318   Consider the *cakor* bird: he lives
      on moonbeams, or sparks from burning coals.
      He craves no third.

319   This isn't a misty drizzle, my friend:
      it's smoke that's rising from the ground
      as early monsoon clouds come burning the earth.

320   Leaving home, her husband left the house
      in that neighbor's care—you should have seen
      the smile that shone through wifely tears.

321   Singed by separation's fires, yet swamped by tears
      and whirling in a wind of sighs,
      her heart survives the nights and days.

322   Ensnared by the thief of hearts, yet bashful
      among her elders, she rides a swing of feelings
      as she does her work about the house.

I've read for sure the vein of womankind: 323
he is the cause of her disease,
he the physician, he the healing herb.[158]

The lady you love and lodge within your heart   324
peeps on tiptoe through your eyes—
and wears me down.

Who can stay stubborn in the rains?   325
While other knots may tighten,
the knot of jealous anger is bound to yield.

Let those who brag about eternal life   326
first brave a moment's separation
in the rains.

She yearns for him, yet their meeting is not to be;   327
repeatedly she hugs them to her heart—
his garments, gems, and weaponry.

My shameless limbs cling joyously to his   328
and bring me shame; like dew at dawn,
my jealous anger leaves unseen.

Your body's grace   329
draws on all the beauty of the world,
drops into my eye, drowns my sight in savor.

49

330 Pray, press in your arms that other girl,
whose name is on your tongue
when you hold me in your embrace.[159]

331 The girl looked, aimed her glancing dart;
then in a flash, she flared, fired,
and fled away.[160]

332 Hand holding hand through a hole in the wall,
they slept the night at ease,
lying as it were in each other's arms.[161]

333 Freed, her flowing hair frees me from the world;
bound, her dark and graceful locks
bind tight my heart.

334 It's spring: there are no hot or chilling winds.
So please tell me: How come your limbs
appear to gleam and tremble so?

335 Through a sheer veil peep gleaming eyes:
paired fishes leaping, bright
in Ganga's limpid stream.

336 So long apart, and yet they live! Thus in their shame
no words will come; with shyly downcast eyes
they run into each other's arms.

The moonlight's hidden, and darkness daubs the earth, 337
but have no fear. Walk on and smile,
moving the mantle from your moon-bright face.

Both lovers long to speak their hearts, 338
but neither finds the words; their speech—
a miser with a beggar at the gate—will not emerge.

When a villain gives up villainy 339
we feel alarmed; a spotless moon
foretells calamity.

Courting death by suffering the pain of love, 340
she runs again the gauntlet of the moon,
the lotus, and the fragrant breeze.[162]

The cooling fan you sent with loving care 341
may ease her body's fire, but in its breeze
how freely she perspires.[163]

Thinking of her lord of life, she's steeped in joy 342
through night and day; she trembles, thrills,
and now and then perspires.

The darkness of separation holds no fears for me, 343
for in my eyes there glows, both night and day,
her flamelike form.

344   Scorched in love's pain, when fireflies came
      she burned again: "Oh, come inside!" she cried.
      "Tonight the sky rains burning coals."

345   Startled by the red flame trees in full bloom,
      an artless traveler thought the forest all afire;
      he turned back on his trail and hurried home.

346   Ensconced within the family, her back was turned;
      and yet there chanced to come my way
      a shy and smiling glance.

347   The other girls all laugh and sing in glee.
      Why then do you alone lament
      as he, your husband's younger brother, weds?[164]

348   This thorn in my foot revived me as I died:
      my dearest's fear in drawing it out
      made clear his love.[165]

349   That very girl, dear Lal,
      who so adorned your brow with lac-stained feet
      was doubtless she whose red lips tinged your eyes.[166]

350   My eyes observe no bounds
      and will not heed the reins of shame;
      like a headstrong steed they forge ahead.

She glimpsed her lover in her mirror ring,   351
and fearlessly, though turned away,
she feasted on his face with steady gaze.

I cannot tell: inhaling hookah smoke,   352
with pursed lips and laughing eyes and brows,
did Lal perhaps inhale my heart as well?

Sidelong glances,   353
sweet as honey in the moment of their meeting,
hurt me now like a scorpion's sting.

She won't be parted from your happy gift, dear Lal: 354
the fragrance of that garland may be lost,
but not its lifelong lease upon her heart.

Smiling with love, the knowing lady called her child;   355
and where her lover's mouth had kissed
she kissed the boy and trembled.

Seeing me, pretending she had not, she made   356
a show of all her limbs, then sat in bashfulness,
withdrawn again.

Feather-clad, with grit for food   357
and winged mate for company, you alone,
oh dove, know happiness in this world.

358   Oh, who's to say? Consider thoughtfully—
      which person and which pond
      remains contained in times of flood?

359   Filled with feeling, love and longing, pining pain,
      a million missives fly between the pair
      as they near the door.

360   Hearing my tread, the bather glanced my way,
      then turned, took fright, shrank back—
      and smiled at me with bashful glance.

361   They clung and parted, clung and parted, clung again;
      at dawn they'd left the house, but the setting sun
      ended their first day's journey at the gate.[167]

362   Peering through half-opened eyes,
      twisting her limbs, stretching, half rising,
      she lies back with a languid yawn.

363   Now here's a sight to charm the mind:
      see how she lingers as she stares,
      her fingers parting the blind.

364   Her lover's note: she grasps it, kisses it, touches it
      to her brow, clasps it to her heart;
      she holds it, reads it, folds it away.

Unveiling her face, he watched as feigned sleep fled: 365
her lips trembled and her body thrilled
as she opened wide her eyes and met his gaze.

Charmed by the charmer of minds, cleave   366
to the cloud-dark, roam with the roamer of the groves,
hold the mountain holder in your heart.[168]

Thinking the trickster slept,   367
I stole up close and kissed his cheek; he laughed,
I shied away; he clasped me, and I clung to him.

The lovers strive to rise at dawn—   368
only to embrace, still half asleep,
and sink back down again.

Natures turn with the turn of time, all quit their course.   369
Even the lord of mercy is merciless
in this ill-begotten age.

Good sense and ageless wisdom testify   370
that while too subtle for a worldly eye
her waist and God both have reality.[169]

Drunk on her body,   371
her lover would drink nothing else: the cup
long lingered at his lip, and on her face his gaze.

372   So cruelly crushed is her blossomlike form, my God!
      Rest a hand on her heart and see,
      is it beating still?

373   So many are Gokul's noble wives, so full of good counsel;
      yet who among them failed to leave her lane
      at the sound of that calling flute?

374   Though lovely, trim, and tapering your form may be,
      the luster of a lamp depends
      on the oil of love lying within its heart.[170]

375   Seeping from eyelids, trickling through lashes,
      coursing down cheeks, her tears fall to her breast,
      sputter for a second, and are gone.[171]

376   As her hand moves, so the yarn; and as the
      yarn moves, so the girl: the skillful spinner
      dances as she spins.

377   Bereft of their husbands' love,
      they noisily parade their married state,
      feigning sleepy eyes and languid limbs.

378   When he's in view I cannot lift my gaze,
      yet not to see him is sheer misery:
      no comfort lies in store for these sad eyes.

So slender the creator made her waist,   379
its being and not being are as one—
though breasts and hips make good the loss.

Revealing it, now touching it, now hiding it away,   380
looking in the mirror at the lip her lover bruised,
she passes her day.

Nothing can relieve my body's fire   381
until like well-drenched garments
my lover's limbs enfold me.

Her fearful pain can be borne no more,   382
recital of her absent lover's name
the only way to sustain her parting soul.

Why fret, poor hart? None can escape this net.   383
The more you struggle to be free,
the more are you entwined.

Now leave all hope of help, the rains have come: 384
to bear the fragrance of *kadamba* flowers
is certainly no game.[172]

Her earring glows with lustrous pearls   385
as though beads of sweat
were seeping at the touch of a tender cheek.

386 His body blends with shadow, hers with moon;
     two souls are one, as Hari and Radha
     roam the lane.[173]

387 Peacock crown, why preen on gaining Krishna's head?
     You'll soon be tumbling to his feet
     when you hear of Radha's wrathful mood.

388 Quite other is your gait, your speech, your glow:
     your angry frowns aside, all this declares
     you've won his heart in recent days.

389 *Bindī* on the brow, lips red with *pān*,
     cascading hair, and kohl-rimmed eyes:
     how finely she shines in natural array.

390 Reflected in the mirror of her lovely limbs,
     twofold, threefold, fourfold seems to be
     her jewelry.

391 Arms raised and turned, long strands in her hands,
     veil thrown back on shoulder—whose heart
     would she not bind as she binds her hair?

392 Cool, fragrant breezes waft through the shade
     of a leafy grove; once more my heart would be
     on that same Yamuna shore.

With dusky loveliness, Shyam's   393
body glows in a golden shawl:
a sapphire mountain in a blazing dawn.

Her slender body fills out   394
with flames of luster licking every limb
so lavishly.

Alike in fragrance, hue, and tenderness,   395
a rosy petal falls upon her cheek
and no one knows.

Against the golden girl it lies disguised;   396
only when it withers is
her jasmine garland seen.

Don't hang the curd pot up! Nor take it down!   397
Stay as you are—just reaching for the hanging net,
you look so fine.

She lifts a hand to veil her face—her sari shifts;   398
joyfully her lover steals a prize
as her belly's furrows meet his eyes.

Many times he walks this lane, but though I try,   399
I cannot train my eyes to look his way.
My longing for a sight of him is in its prime.

400   There, princely son of Nand—
      it's all well done, I swear,
      if you look kindly on my deed.[174]

NOTES

1   This opening paean to Radha, with its striking chromatic imagery (her golden color blends with Krishna's blue to produce a verdant green), replaces the traditional encomium to Ganesh as the remover of any obstacles in the poet's intended path.

2   The implication is that the girl has no control over the physical and psychological changes that she experiences as she matures; rather, they are controlled by a despotic and passionate monarch, youth.

3   Her fair complexion hides the heroine in moonlight as she heads for a tryst, but her natural fragrance gives her away.

4   In this companion piece to the previous couplet, the heroine expresses alarm at the possibility of her moonlit exposure.

5   The heroine's complexion outshines the white jasmine garland, which seems yellowish by contrast.

6   Vishnu's rescue of an elephant from the jaws of a crocodile is a standard salvific image from the Purana tradition.

7   This depiction of emotions subverts the trope of a boat crossing the ocean of life. In a parallel trope of the mind as a boat turning on a single point, the yogic desideratum of "stilling the mind" is ironically achieved by enchantment.

8   Since physical contact is impossible, the heroine consoles herself (and thrills her lover) by making their shadows touch.

9   The heroine's eyes are so elegantly elongated that they "seek union" with the ears.

10   Duryodhana, "undefeatable warrior," was a Kuru prince and protagonist of the *Mahābhārata*. He felt simultaneous delight and pain as he died, which is emphasized in vernacular tradition. Soham Pain kindly provided the reference to Kashiramdas's Bengali *Sauptikaparva*, in which "the king gave up his body in joy and grief" (Kashiramadasa 2014: 875).

11   A *thag*, or highway robber, befriends and then ritually murders his victims in the "false dawn" of a moonlit night; see the real-world narrative in *Ardhakathānaka* 412 (Chowdhury 2009: 170) for just such a false dawn. Like many of Bihari's more elaborate narratives, the actions here are relayed in flashback.

12   Displaced cosmetics betray passionate lovemaking.

13 Although translated as "compass," the device referenced here is more specifically the *kabilanamā*, for Persian *qibla-numā*, an instrument that indicates the direction of the Ka'ba in Mecca.

14 The heroine's husband returns after making love to another woman, as suggested by his unsteady gait.

15 Unusually, this couplet places Krishna in a courtly setting and refers to the heroine as an unnamed lady.

16 The heroine's heels have a natural redness, indicating delicacy.

17 Tradition has it that this verse was used to stir the conscience of Maharaja Jai Singh, the poet's patron, when he became obsessed with a young girl.

18 The word *agani*, translated as "fire," may also mean "uncountable."

19 The beauty of the young bride makes her a threat to her older co-wives.

20 The phrase translated as "God reveals the world entire" has two connotations: God has both "made the world known" and "made the known world."

21 The mole on the heroine's face equates to the spot on the moon.

22 There is a pun on the barber's wife losing her footing as she applies lac to the lady's feet but finds them already red like the *kaũhara* vine.

23 The woman is covering her face with the edge of her sari.

24 This celebration of the beauty of the heroine's face is based on the poetic figure *pratīpa*, wherein reality outstrips conventional similes; the lotus and the moon are two such poetic standards for female beauty.

25 The flying of paper kites from rooftops is a popular pastime and an everyday image.

26 "Raghurai" is King of the Raghus, Ram. The poet sarcastically deconstructs his divine epithets "friend of the poor" (*dīnabandhu*) and "savior" (*tāraka*), respectively.

27 Gathering clouds foreshadow the season when lovers are supposed to be together but cannot be united.

28 While Kanha (Krishna) is not normally associated with *dāna*, giving, his persona as Vishnu fills that role.

29 The poem refers to the silken cloth known in Hindi as *dhūp-chāh̃*, "sun-and-shade," whose complementary colors in the warp and the woof yield a shimmering effect.

30   The moonlike luster of the heroine's face makes it impossible to tell the phase of the real moon in her vicinity.

31   The heroine's eyes, nimble and tremulous, are likened to a wagtail bird with black and white tail feathers that twitch rapidly up and down and produce a flashing effect. A "wagtail-eyed" woman is a popular description of beauty. Nandkumar, "son of Nand," is Krishna.

32   His forehead is smeared with lac from the feet of a rival beloved. The word translated here as "deny" can also mean "mirror."

33   The word *lākhanu* appears twice in the couplet. Trying to save Bihari from the rhetorical fault of repetition, Ratnakar holds that the first *lākhanu* ("lakhs are bettered . . .") may be the name of some adversary of Jai Singh (here called Jai Shah).

34   In this verse, Kamdev is presented as a Maina tribesman. The Maina or Mina are a tribal people of Rajasthan who were feared because of their often fierce opposition to Rajput hegemony. The original builders and defenders of a fortress at Amber, they were ousted by the Kachhwaha dynasty in the twelfth century.

35   The *guñja* berry (also called *cuhaṭanī*, the clinger) is threaded for simple necklaces and also used to preserve camphor.

36   The forehead mark is of *aipan*, a rice-and-turmeric paste used to decorate pots during festivals; it is an image of domesticity and simple charm.

37   The original couplet begins with a list of life's pleasures in pairs of two-word compounds.

38   The crocodile-shaped earring stands for Kamdev, who has accessed Krishna's heart through the ear (i.e., through speech).

39   The trembling of the earring suggests the heroine's state of mental and physical excitement. The "white veil" alludes to the pale color attributed to the Ganges.

40   In the summer month of Jeth, the days lengthen in proportion to the shortening nights; similarly, in adolescence, the breasts fill out in proportion to the shrinking of the waist.

41   The sound the heroine makes is the "pop" of a flame as it goes out.

42   The loud noise and pomp of the large ceremonial kettledrum (*damāmau*) is associated with the affairs of "the great."

43   The garland worn by Lal the night before, wilted after their lovemaking.

44 White jasmine and dark *tamāla* tree suggest the limbs of the heroine and hero, respectively.

45 English requires gendered pronouns, but the two protagonists in this pastoral verse are not gendered in the original couplet, emphasizing the fullness of the union.

46 The (grammatically feminine) waist bells and (masculine) anklets both have an element of gendered personification in the original couplet.

47 The heroine quenched the flame of both the lamp and the hero's lust.

48 An implicit invitation to a lover to step inside, this verse describes the contracting shadows of noon in Jeth (May–June) and reflects *Gāthāsaptaśati* I.49, whose wording may inform the first line of this couplet. See Introduction, pp. xiv–xv.

49 The heroine's fair complexion makes her invisible among the jasmine flowers in the wood, where she has gone to meet her lover, but her fragrance gives her away.

50 As crops are harvested, trysting places disappear.

51 After a long absence, the hero returns to his beloved; the short closing stage of the journey seems interminable. The word *gvaïṛau* ("cattle track" or "purlieu") is from the reconstructed Sanskrit *godaṇḍa* ("cow path").

52 Since the month of Pūs (December–January) is a good time for travel, the heroine plays *Malār*, a monsoon raga or musical mode, and thus evokes (or provokes) the rains—making it a season for staying home.

53 The word for birdlime, *caïpu*, can also mean "a gummy secretion (in the eye)" (McGregor 1993: 328); it here implies both "to shine" and "to be smeared, be sticky."

54 The yellow of the saffron suggests the heroine's fairness and is contrasted to the lake waters.

55 The husband's playfulness with his new bride incites jealousy in his other wives.

56 According to a story in the Puranas, the dwarf incarnation of Vishnu is granted three dwarfish strides' worth of land by the demon king Bali. He assumes his universal form and covers the three worlds in his three steps, winning the whole of creation back from demonic forces. To grasp the wrist is to make an aggressive overture.

57 While Krishna is inherent within the soul as "inner controller" (*antaryāmī*), paradoxically he is also immanent in the world.

58 The imperfections of "blemished glass" refract light from the emphatically singular form of God into the numerous visible forms of the universe. The couplet simultaneously celebrates and excoriates the phenomenal world: it is not ultimately "true," perhaps, but its very limitations reflect the divine. In the closing foot of the original couplet, Bihari uses Sanskrit, vernacular, and Persianate words—manifesting the entirety of his lexicon, and through it, the entire "created world" referenced here.

59 The description is of Krishna the dancer (*naṭa*, also "tumbler," "actor"), who wears the telltale crown featured in his iconography. Krishna walks with a capricious, carefree gait, suggested by a trisyllabic cadence in the original couplet—the opposite of a normative foursquare marching beat.

60 The lover's letter is a dagger to slay the beloved's *viraha*, or lovesickness, so she holds it to her heart, where *viraha* resides.

61 The couplet describes the "mirror hall" in Jai Singh's palace at Amber, which makes a whole regiment of its reflected hero. The conceit rests on the commonplace metaphor of lovemaking as battle.

62 The hero implies that the heroine's blush attests to a night of love, and she implies the same about him. In the original couplet, the hero's question is agentless (literally, "what redness has come about?"), suggesting that he is deliberately assuming an innocent explanation.

63 The very seasons contrive against her, intensifying her *viraha* and depriving her of solitude in which to mourn his absence privately.

64 A cold winter's day is a novelty for a short time only, just like the visit of a son-in-law.

65 The *sakhī* advises the heroine as the cowherds leave the platforms where the villagers assemble to herd the cows home. The word translated as "dust" means both the dust from the hooves of the cows and an evening haze in which dust seems to rise from the earth itself.

66 A colorful *bindī*, or forehead mark, would show clearly on the heroine's fair brow, but a mark of sandalwood (suggesting piety) remains invisible until her complexion is reddened (and her piety diluted) by wine.

67 The original couplet has a high, Sanskrit register, and only the first half of the second line is truly vernacular. The gown is a loose, flowing kurta or shift; its fine cloth allows only a filtered vision of the fingernail scratch, just as water in a bowl imperfectly reflects the young moon. The "new moon" reference alludes conventionally to the crescent-shaped mark made on skin by a lover's fingernail.

68 The couplet begins with "*bālamu bāraī*," literally "the lover, at the time [of the rival wife]," an echo of the Sanskritic adverb *bārambāra* ("over and over"), giving an extra spin to the merry-go-round of these wild domestic arrangements.

69 The poem is a conventional description of adolescent beauty and a remarkable statement about poetic meaning, which, like the girl's budding breasts just discernible ("barely concealed") under her bodice and damp sari, lies almost hidden under ornament and allusion. In both cases, the outer shape gives only a general impression of inner beauty.

70 The heroine's body outshines her bright clothing, negating its purpose as a covering.

71 Lovers prevented by society from meeting or speaking to each other must communicate through the eyes alone; "rooftops" signifies the open rooftop terraces from which neighbors can gaze at each other.

72 The hero ascribes to the woman's *sakhī* the sensual approach of the woman herself.

73 The military terminology is Mughal.

74 Krishna being dark and Radha fair, their "radiance" in the second line of the Braj Bhasha verse represents the respective colors of the Yamuna and Ganga rivers, whose mingling at Prayag (modern Allahabad, or Prayagraj) makes this river confluence the acme of pilgrimage sites. The poem shows how a devotional attitude can subvert or invert religious hierarchies.

75 The victim here is a lady who has not yet recovered from lovesickness, the speaker is a *sakhī,* and the addressee is the uncaring hero.

76 The conceit is that the "love god" assumes the role of the creator, Brahma, to fashion the heroine's thighs from nothing but beauty. The trunks of banana or plantain trees are a traditional simile for female thighs.

77 The heroine cannot resist the chaotic physical changes associated

with the onset of maturity, likened to a palace coup that promotes "small to great" and turns "great to small."

78 A fluttering sensation in the eye (left for a woman, right for a man) is a happy omen.

79 The vestibule (*baroṭhā*) or doorway is the location for a welcome ceremony for a bridegroom.

80 The cooling moon is a source of the "heat" of anguish for separated lovers.

81 The couplet brazenly mocks Krishna, "lord of *gopīs*," who will lose his heart at the sight of a girl's pretty hands (implicitly Radha's).

82 Clad in chains and cowrie necklace, the archetypal Afghan *malaṅg* ascetic has a single-minded concentration on God, his beloved.

83 A *sakhī* prepares the heroine for a tryst.

84 Addressing a *sakhī,* a heroine, pained by her lover's absence, reinterprets the moonlight, unwilling to concede its usual happy associations.

85 The singular, united beauty of Radha and Krishna is contrasted with the need for multiple eyes to appreciate their joint form.

86 A *sakhī* advises the heroine not to fall for a new (rival) admirer.

87 Showing standard Vaishnava piety, the supplicant rates the concept of closeness to Hari (Vishnu-Krishna) superior to salvation.

88 The "summerhouse" has walls of dampened matted grass that has a cooling effect when a breeze blows.

89 Traditionally, a woman is allowed a certain social intimacy with her husband's younger brother, who is closer to her in age than her older husband. See also v. 347. The welts are a reaction to the brother-in-law's romantic attentions, but the innocent *sakhīs* treat them as an illness.

90 Translated here as "daisy chain," *pabhulā* and its variant *pahulā* are obscure, but seem to mean a wildflower adornment of a village belle.

91 The *gopī* is devoted to Krishna alone, and has ears only for the sound of his flute. The subtlety of the poem lies in not mentioning either protagonist by name and leaving the context as a matter of inference.

92 By refusing to name or specify his subjects (except as *doū,* "both, the two"), Bihari leaves the reader as much in the dark as the protagonists themselves.

93 There is no true present tense in the original poem.

94 "Heron," literally *kulaṅga,* a species of crane.

95 The protagonists here are the Mishra (Brahman exegete) and his clandestine beloved.

96 Lovemaking has inverted the "proper" position of betel-nut stains and kohl on the errant lover's face. Much of the humor in this sarcastic poem comes from the contrast between the conservative opening proverb and the hero's appearance.

97 "Nonday in the almanac" is a lunar day that exists in theory but has no practical existence due to incompatibility with the solar calendar.

98 The heroine is burning with the fire of love in separation from her lover.

99 The verse expresses desire for union with Krishna by the devotee, whose heart has endured every kind of suffering. The "triple fires" (literally *traitāpa,* threefold burning, pain, suffering) may refer to the three modes of human suffering: *ādhibhautika* (from worldly causes), *ādhidaivika* (from divine causes), and *ādhyātmika* (from spiritual causes); rhetorically, the verse stresses the broad context of suffering endured in the world, as a foil to the longed-for intimacy of divine comfort.

100 Lac on a woman's feet indicates her married state, which is already a challenge to the rival wife. To discover that the husband himself applied it adds insult to injury.

101 "The lifting of the bridal veil" is the introduction of a new bride to the household, a ritual of crossing the threshold when the members of her new family greet her with gifts. The poem captures the bittersweet quality of the last of the three gifts: the *suhāga* (marital happiness, auspicious state of being married) until now enjoyed by her co-wives, who know that they cannot compete with her fresh charms.

102 The Yamuna invokes Krishna because of its conventionally dark color, implicit here. In a controlled hyperbole, Radha's tears are profuse enough to turn the Yamuna's fresh water brackish—but only for a moment and only at the river's edge.

103 The stereotypically mean father-in-law has appointed the young bride the family almsgiver at the door of the household, but he has overlooked the fact that her daintiness may prove as charming to the wider world as it was meant to be economical to him.

104 Harihara is a joint form of Vishnu and Shiva. Hari/Vishnu bears

Lakshmi in his heart; Hara/Shiva bears a crescent moon on his forehead. The epithets are reengineered in a caustic description of the unfaithful lover, with his inward obsession and outward scratch marks.

105   The lover has scratched the heroine in a passionate farewell embrace.

106   "Biharilal," a name of Krishna meaning "darling wanderer [in the groves]" and also the name of the poet, appears here as a poetic signature.

107   The sidelong glance, shot from the arched "bow" of the eyebrow, is a stock weapon in love's armory. Bihari specifies the association between bow and arrow as one of cause and effect.

108   The hero, deprived in public of closeness to his beloved—or estranged from her for some reason—suffers at the sight of the lighthearted happiness she enjoys with her female friends.

109   The allusion is to a wildfire that Krishna swallowed when it threatened Braj, and, of course, to the emotions burning his heart.

110   The transience of a husband's affections is as sure as the transience of the seasons; Jeṭh and Māh are summer and winter months, respectively. "Momentary married bliss" includes the meaning "agreement, contract, circumstance" (*samaya*).

111   "Teej": during the *tīja paraba*, a feast on the third day of the month Sāvan in early August, married women make offerings for the well-being of their husbands. In this couplet, the co-wives dress up in their finery for the festival; but the "morning-after" appearance of their rival, the young bride, tells of her night with their shared husband.

112   "Obliquity" is the common quality that links this list of nine seemingly disparate items. The allusions are as follows: fort defenses should be obliquely angled to inhibit frontal attacks by the enemy; eyelashes and locks of hair should curl for maximal charm; eyebrows should be coquettishly arched, the better to fire their glance arrows—in the manner of an archer's bow, which likewise should curve well; young women should have curves in all the right places and, in the abstract sense of "obliqueness," should also be a little "arch"; a horse should have the requisite curvature between shoulder and rump; and rapidly sung musical phrases should double back on themselves repeatedly, zigzagging in their rapid ascent and descent of the scale.

113   This conceit has the heroine so grievously emaciated by lovesickness

that the intake and expulsion of sighs is enough to throw her forward and backward respectively. The rhetorically superfluous measurement of the ground covered by her movements ("six or seven cubits") roots this conceit in a certain reality: she's blown about a lot, but not beyond measurability. The image of the swing, normally associated with playfulness and joy, is a cruel irony for the grief-stricken heroine.

114 Dazed by love and lovemaking, the heroine walks unsteadily. This unsteadiness is wryly interpreted as deriving from the "weight" of her innate beauty, leading to a contemplation of the extra weight of ornaments—which would only detract from her already perfect beauty.

115 Just as a zero multiplies to the power of ten, so the zerolike forehead mark augments the heroine's beauty. The translation "beyond all telling" targets the old sense of "counting" as well as the newer sense of "communicating information."

116 The singeing is from the heroine's burning hands; under the circumstances, she could not write anything, but sent the letter anyway.

117 "Thornbush": *javāsa* is a thorny shrub whose leaves fall in the monsoon.

118 Gold ornaments add nothing to the heroine's already perfect body, merging invisibly into the glow of her golden (or "wheaten") complexion.

119 A perfumed "balm" is applied to the body after bathing, but like all artificial beautification, it can only detract from the heroine—it "dulls the mirror." "Breath" (*usāsu*) also suggests a sigh.

120 "Fine white," *pacatoriyā:* a cloth so lightweight that a sari made of it weighs only five *tolās,* i.e., a few grams. "Waterfall's cascade," *jala cādara:* a cascading "sheet of water," used in the cooling and decorating of Mughal and Rajput palaces.

121 This couplet adds graphic detail to the previous one, but personifies "warmth" itself as a refugee from the cold of winter.

122 A red powder thrown about in Holi celebrations.

123 This couplet resonates with v. 257, with which it shares rhyme words. It conveys a mood of impatient longing: what might have been a merely sententious verse ("open your heart to God") is lent depth of feeling by an ambiguity in which Hari's desired access to the enclosure of the heart suggests a lover at the threshold. In the second line of the original couplet, harsh alliteration suggests the

thud and grate of a door locking; in the translation, this is imitated but altered by the scratchier, more metallic monosyllables ("latch, bolt, lock, tight").

124 When the heroine's golden luster lends her pearls a yellowish glow, the *sakhī* thinks them amber, and tests their electrostatic attraction with a blade of grass.

125 Kite: see v. 38, n. 25.

126 The heroine fancies the pigeon fancier.

127 The couplet's technical register reflects the process of distillation, with tears as the distilled product.

128 Rosary: the *mālā* or *japa mālā* is used when reciting the names of God.

129 The heroine is lightninglike in the intermittent way that she "flashes" (glows with excitement) and shelters in the hero's (cloud-dark) limbs.

130 The "oozing" refers to the secretion of a sticky liquid from the side of an elephant's head during musth.

131 The heroine addresses the suspect hero.

132 This couplet's imagery comes from the building technique of "falsework": the *kālbūt* (Persian *kālbud*), "support," is a temporary frame or "centering" of bricks and mortar or timber that supports a stone arch under construction. Similarly, the go-between brings about a relationship between lovers, acting as the temporary frame to prop up the first delicate connections of the arch.

133 Ram crossed the sea to Lanka on a stone causeway, and can take the devotee across the ocean of the world.

134 Krishna bears the lotuslike heroine within his heart, and fears oppressing her there with the weight of his conventional chest adornments, each tied to one of his epithets: a balm of camphor (*ghana*), suggesting "cloud-dark" (*ghanasyāma*); sandalwood (*candanu*), suggesting "Krishna of the lunar dynasty" (*kṛṣṇacandra*); and a wildflower garland (*banamāla*), suggesting "the forest-garlanded" (*banamālī*).

135 The couplet implies that the heroine's beauty, superior to jewels, is likely to draw many pairs of roving eyes.

136 A *sakhī* suggests that the heroine should complete her (false) display of jealous anger by concealing the loving look in her eyes.

137 "The glow of lips and eyes and sash": conventionally, lips are red (with betel juice); eyes are dark; Krishna's clothing is yellow.

138 The indeterminate quality of narrator and subject allows the verse

to be read as either romantic/erotic or spiritual/devotional—as in v. 226, whose rhyme words this couplet shares.

139 *Hari:* both vocative (as translated), and "being defeated."

140 This poem celebrates the quality of crookedness, rakishness, and a willful "inclination" toward unconventional behavior. In confessing such characteristics to Krishna, the poet-narrator simultaneously boasts of them, confident that they reflect and match Krishna's own "deviant" character. "Three curves" refers to Krishna's "thrice-bent" flute-playing pose with bent neck, waist, and knee—which could only be accommodated by a suitably "bent" or "crooked" receptacle. The couplet is an implicit invitation to Krishna to dwell in the poet's heart.

141 The word translated as "string" (*guna*) connotes both the "quality" of a qualified deity (whose deeds are portrayed in imaginative narratives, hence "yarns"), and a string as on a kite (see v. 38, n. 25).

142 The incongruity between rose blooms and the thorny branches of the rosebush is a poetic commonplace. Bihari uses it to comment on the fickleness of fate and on incongruous associations or rewards generally.

143 "To seize one's passing shade": a reference to *chāyāgrāhiṇī* ("shadow grasper"), a demoness in the Ramayana who tried to impede Hanuman as he crossed the ocean to Lanka.

144 The changing seasons suggest a broader pattern of changing fortunes. Verse 262 shares an almost identical final quarter-verse, suggesting that both verses may have been composed in a *samasyā-pūrti* format (in which the poet improvises a verse around a given line or part line).

145 Another couplet deriding provinciality. The three professions all depend traditionally on donkeys, not elephants, for their freight transport (the much-maligned donkey is referenced implicitly).

146 The heroine is so emaciated through lovesickness that the betel juice she drinks is visible through her slender neck.

147 In currency conventions, a curved line graphically distinguished a rupee from a *dāma,* a unit of smaller denomination.

148 The heroine reads telltale marks on the hero's chest, where her rival's necklace has left its trace upon the skin. The couplet rests on the punning potential of the word *guna,* meaning both "quality" and "thread" (of a necklace or garland); see v. 260, n. 141.

149 While the young heroine's chest bears the weight of her breasts, the rival co-wives feel oppressed by her new charms.

150 A secret love affair is exposed when the lover goes away; the milk bush plant yields a milky sap that can be used as "invisible ink," showing up when heated.

151 Personified emotions are subject to their own characteristics: shyness feels shy while boldness acts boldly.

152 In the original couplet, the portrayal of the heroine's contentment contains nine occurrences of the consonant *k*. Strongly indicative of action in Indic languages, this sound appears three times in each of the first three quarter-verses but is suddenly absent in the fourth.

153 Arrow cage: a tightly fitting cage with spikes to impale the prisoner.

154 The male *cakavā* and female *cakaī* are said to call mournfully to each other during their mythic nighttime separation.

155 "Fiery June winds": north India's hot summer wind.

156 Hari (Vishnu) holds Lakshmi within his heart; Hara (Shiva) and Parvati are often depicted as the complementary halves of a single form.

157 Inversions of emotion beset the lovesick, for whom the remembered associations of comfortable things transform them into a source of torment.

158 The word translated as "vein" can also mean "woman."

159 A betrayed heroine sarcastically berates her unfaithful lover; the original couplet reaches an alliterative crescendo with his name, "Lala."

160 A momentary glance from the heroine smites the hero. The "dart" is like a crossbow bolt, but is fired in volleys from a *nāvaka*, a gunlike weapon.

161 Neighboring lovers have only hand contact (through a hole in the wall separating their two houses) during the night.

162 "The moon, the lotus, and the fragrant breeze" are reminiscent of happier romantic times, and therefore conventionally painful to the lovesick (see v. 303, n. 157). In exposing herself to them, the heroine seeks to increase her pain until it kills her.

163 The fan sent by the heroine's lover does cool her, but its status as a gift from him also fans her passion, and she is bathed in sweat.

164 See v. 155, n. 89.

165 The pain from a thorn in her foot was killing her, but when she saw

the tenderness with which her lover drew it out, the pain became a blessing.

166 Red eyes are evidence of nightlong lovemaking.

167 The lovers' reluctance to part means that the whole day passes in simply crossing the courtyard.

168 The epithets all pertain to Krishna.

169 The heroine's waist is compared to God: both are subtle and invisible, yet assumed to exist based on "good sense" and "ageless wisdom" (*śruti,* literally "that which is heard," the "revealed scripture" or the Veda). Just as the phenomenal world could not exist without God as root cause, the heroine's body could not exist without a waist to join its upper and lower portions. Compare v. 379.

170 This couplet puns on the multiple meanings of the word *guna* (Sanskrit *guṇa*), which include "lamp wick" as well as "having qualities" (see v. 260, n. 141). The heroine's glowing body is likened to the lamp itself, both "imbued with qualities" and "having a wick."

171 The fevered breast of the heroine is like a hot griddle to her falling tears.

172 The rains end hopes of travel, and hence hopes of reunion; the monsoon-flowering *kadamba* tree (burflower) symbolizes this seasonal change.

173 Dusky Krishna and fair Radha are concealed, respectively, by the shade and light on a moonlit lane overhung with trees; they seem as one because only one of them is visible at any time. Bihari updates the conventional conceit of Radha and Krishna being one soul in two bodies.

174 In no other edition does this couplet have final position, but it provides an apt conclusion to our text.

GLOSSARY

BIHARILAL (*bihārīlāla*) the darling playful one, Krishna (and the name of the poet)

BRAJ (*braja*) the realm of Krishna's childhood, associated with the Yamuna River, a cowherding community, the Govardhan Hill, and pleasant groves

GOKUL (*gokula*) the village in Braj where Krishna spent part of his childhood

GOPAL (*gopāla*) "the cowherd," Krishna

gopī one of the cowherd girls with whom Krishna played love games in Braj

HARI Krishna/Vishnu, God

JADUPATI "Lord of the Yadus," Krishna

JAI SHAH Jai Singh I (1611–1667), Biharilal's patron, raja of Amber and a general (entitled "Mirza") in the Mughal army

KAMDEV (*kāmadeva*) the god of love

KRISHNA (*kṛṣṇa*) "the dark one," an incarnation of the god Vishnu; his precocious childhood and adolescence was spent among the cowherds of Braj, where Radha became his lover

LAL (*lāla*) dear boy, darling; Krishna

MOHAN (*mohana*) "the enchanting one," Krishna

pān betel leaf packed with slaked lime and other ingredients, chewed as a stimulant or digestive

RADHA (*rādhā*) diminutive Radhika, Krishna's lover, his favorite among the *gopīs* (in later theology, developed into a major goddess)

sakhī a woman's intimate female companion or confidante, who acts as go-between serving the romance of lover and beloved

SHYAM (*śyāma*) "the dark one," Krishna

SHYAMGHAN (*śyāmaghana*) "dark cloud," Krishna

BIBLIOGRAPHY

Editions and Translations

Bihari. 1896. *The Satsaiya of Bihari, with a Commentary Entitled the Lala-Candrika by Çri Lallu Lal Kavi*. Edited by G. A. Grierson. Calcutta: The Superintendent of Government Printing.

———. 1990. *The Satasaī*. Translated by K. P. Bahadur. Delhi: Penguin.

———. 2002. *The Bihārī-Satasaī*. Translated by Satya Dev Choudhary. Mumbai: Bharatiya Vidya Bhavan.

———. N.d. *Bihārī vibhūti*. Edited by Ramkumari Mishra. Allahabad: Lokbharati Prakashan.

Biharidas. 2008. *Satsaī*. Edited by Lakshmidhar Malaviya. 3 vols. Delhi: Aditya Prakashan.

Holland, Barron. 1970. "The Satsaī of Bihārī: Hindi Poetry of the Early Rīti Period." Unpublished PhD dissertation. Berkeley: University of California.

Jagannathdas "Ratnakar." 1969. *Bihārī-Ratnākar arthāt Bihārī-Satsaī par Ratnākarī ṭīkā*. 5th new ed. Varanasi: Granth-kār.

Jayadeva. 1977. *Love Song of the Dark Lord: Jayadeva's Gītagovinda*. Trans. Barbara Stoler Miller. New York: Columbia University Press.

Jha, Amar Nath. 1973. *The Veiled Moon: Translations of Bihari Satsai*. Edited by Girija Kumar Mathur. New Delhi: Indian Council for Cultural Relations.

Other Sources

Banarasidas. 2009. *Ardhakathanak: A Half Story*. Translated by Rohini Chowdhury. Delhi: Penguin.

Busch, Allison. 2010. "Hidden in Plain View: Brajbhasha Poets at the Mughal Court." *Modern Asian Studies* 44, 2: 267–309.

———. 2011. *Poetry of Kings: The Classical Hindi Literature of Mughal India*. New York: Oxford University Press.

Gerow, Edwin. 1971. *A Glossary of Indian Figures of Speech*. The Hague: Mouton.

Goswamy, B. N. 1997. *Nainsukh of Guler: A Great Indian Painter from a Small Hill-State*. Zurich: Museum Rietberg.

Hala. 1971. *The Prākrit Gāthā-saptaśatī Compiled by Sātavāhana King*

Hāla. Edited and translated by Radhagovind Basak. Calcutta: The Asiatic Society.

———. 1991. *The Absent Traveller: Prākrit Love Poetry from the Gāthāsaptaśatī of Sātavāhana Hāla.* Translated by Arvind Krishna Mehrotra. Delhi: Ravi Dayal.

———. 2009. *Poems on Life and Love in Ancient India: Hāla's Sattasaī.* Translated by Peter Khoroche and Herman Tieken. Albany: State University of New York Press.

Jagannathdas "Ratnakar." 1953. *Kavivar Bihārī.* Edited by Ramakrishna. Varanasi: Granth-kār.

Jayadeva. 1977. *Love Song of the Dark Lord: Jayadeva's Gītagovinda,* trans. Barbara Stoler Miller. New York: Columbia University Press.

Kashiramadasa. 2014. *Sacitra Aṣṭādaśaparva Mahābhārata.* Kolkata: Dey's Publishing.

Maxwell, Glyn. 2013. *On Poetry.* Cambridge, Mass.: Harvard University Press.

McGregor, R. S. 1968. *The Language of Indrajit of Orchā: A Study of Early Braj Bhāṣā Prose.* London: Cambridge University Press.

———. 1984. *Hindi Literature from Its Beginnings to the Nineteenth Century.* Wiesbaden: Harrassowitz.

———. 1993. *Oxford Hindi-English Dictionary.* Oxford: Oxford University Press.

McLeod, W. H. 1976. *The Evolution of the Sikh Community: Five Essays.* Oxford: Clarendon Press.

Miltner, Vladimír. 1961. "Words of Arabic, Persian and Turkish Origin in the Braj Satsaī." *Archiv Orientální* XXIX : 658–659.

———. 1962. "Old Braj Morphology in the Bihārī Satsaī." *Archiv Orientální* XXX: 494–504.

———. 1963. "The Musical Character of the Verses of Bihārīlāl." *Archiv Orientální* XXXI: 216–224.

Platts, John T. 1977. *A Dictionary of Urdū, Classical Hindī, and English.* New Delhi: Oriental Books.

Pollock, Sheldon, trans. and ed. 2016. *A Rasa Reader: Classical Indian Aesthetics.* New York: Columbia University Press.

Rākeśagupta. 1967. *Studies in Nāyaka-Nāyikā Bheda.* Aligarh: Granthayan.

Snell, Rupert. 1991. *The Hindi Classical Tradition: A Braj Bhāṣā Reader.* London: School of Oriental and African Studies.

———. 1994. "Bhakti versus Rīti? The *Satsaī* of Bihārīlāl." *Journal of*

Vaishnava Studies 3, 1: 153-170.

———. 2005. "Confessions of a 17th-Century Jain Merchant: The Ardhakathānak of Banārasīdās." *South Asia Research* 25, 1: 79-104.

Śrīmad Bhāgavata Purāṇa. 2003. *Krishna: The Beautiful Legend of God (Śrīmad Bhāgavata Purāṇa, Book X).* Translated and edited by Edwin F. Bryant. London: Penguin.

Tulsidas. 2016-2023. *The Epic of Ram, vols. 1-7.* Translated by Philip Lutgendorf. Murty Classical Library of India. Cambridge, Mass.: Harvard University Press.

Turner, R. L. 1962-1966. *A Comparative Dictionary of Indo-Aryan Languages.* London: Oxford University Press. [Online version at *http://dsal.uchicago.edu/dictionaries/soas/* incorporates three separately printed supplements, published 1969-1985.]

Vaudeville, Charlotte. 1974. *Kabir.* Oxford: Clarendon Press.